Paragraphs
for
High School

Paragraphs
for
High School

A Sentence-Composing Approach

A Student Worktext

Don and Jenny Killgallon

HEINEMANN
Portsmouth, NH

Heinemann
361 Hanover Street
Portsmouth, NH 03801–3912
www.heinemann.com

Offices and agents throughout the world

Library of Congress Cataloging-in-Publication Data
Killgallon, Don.
   Paragraphs for high school : a sentence-composing approach : a student worktext / Don Killgallon and Jenny Killgallon.
      p. cm.
   Includes bibliographical references.
   ISBN 978-0-325-04253-4 — ISBN 0-325-04253-5
   1. English language—Paragraphs—Problems, exercises, etc.   2. English language—Sentences—Problems, exercises, etc.   3. English language—Rhetoric—Problems, exercises, etc.   4. Report writing—Problems, exercises, etc.   I. Killgallon, Jenny.   II. Title.

PE1439.K55 2012
428.0071'2—dc23   2011047786

Editor: Tobey Antao
Production: Vicki Kasabian
Interior and cover designs: Monica Ann Crigler
Typesetter: Cape Cod Compositors, Inc.
Manufacturing: Steve Bernier

Printed in the United States of America on acid-free paper
16   15   14   13   12   VP   1   2   3   4   5

To Judy, our faithful friend who has stood with us from the beginning, our biggest fan and best critic, our interlocutor on first-Mondays (Jen-Jen) and third-Mondays (Mr. Killgallon), our heart-sister—this one's for you, with love.

CONTENTS

A writer is not someone who expresses thoughts, passion or imagination
in sentences but someone who thinks sentences.
A Sentence-Thinker.

—Roland Barthes, *writer*

THE SENTENCE-COMPOSING APPROACH

Nothing is more satisfying than to write a good sentence.

—Barbara Tuchman, *historian*

THE SENTENCE-PARAGRAPH LINK   1

Sentences unfold one part at a time. Paragraphs unfold one sentence at a time. In this section, authors become your invisible teachers in an apprenticeship in the sentence-composing approach to building better sentences for better paragraphs. Here you'll start becoming a Sentence-Thinker.

BUILDING BETTER SENTENCES

When you have made a new sentence, or even an image that works well,
it is a palace where language itself has lit a new lamp.

—Pat Conroy, *My Reading Life*

BEST SENTENCES   4

A sentence must have a subject (topic) and a predicate (comment about the subject). Best sentences always have something more: sentence parts that are tools to build better sentences like those written by authors.

SHOW ME HOW: SENTENCES   17

Imitating how authors build their sentences focuses on how they write and helps you write in similar ways.

SENTENCE-COMPOSING TOOLS FOR BETTER PARAGRAPHS   32

Writing is carpentry with sentences and paragraphs. Like any craft, it is only as good as the plans, materials, and tools. Here you will learn, practice, and use in paragraphs tools that foster elaboration. All of them are used frequently by your mentor-authors, who will guide you in learning how to use them in your own writing.

THE IDENTIFIER   35

THE ELABORATOR   50

THE DESCRIBER   67

THE COMBO   85

MORE TOOLS   104

GOOD MARKS   112

In punctuating sentences, effective writers go beyond periods and commas. Learning other punctuation marks expands the ways you can express your ideas in sentences in your paragraphs.

BUILDING BETTER PARAGRAPHS

*The practice of professional writers gives no support to the classroom notion
that the paragraph should end with a clincher.*

—Francis Christensen, "A Generative Rhetoric of the Paragraph"

BEST PARAGRAPHS   137

A paragraph contains two or more sentences linked because they are about a common topic. Best paragraphs always have something else: sentence-composing tools like the ones used by authors.

SHOW ME HOW: PARAGRAPHS   141

Imitating how authors build their paragraphs focuses on how they write and helps you write in similar ways.

IMITATING PARAGRAPHS   151

Activities here help you learn how to compose better paragraphs by imitating the experts. Paragraphs by authors give you a blueprint for composing well-built paragraphs.

UNSCRAMBLING PARAGRAPHS   173

Good paragraphs arrange content in ways that make sense to your readers. Unscrambling paragraphs to produce a meaningful arrangement is good practice for composing coherent paragraphs.

BUILDING PARAGRAPHS   184

Here you'll practice how to assemble the raw material for a paragraph into a well-built paragraph. Activities provide practice in how to compose paragraphs through more elaboration and stronger expression of content.

PARTNERING WITH A PRO   204

Throughout, you will have imitated the sentences and paragraphs of pros as your mentors. Now you'll go beyond imitating to create paragraphs with pros as your partners, using the tools for sentences and paragraphs you learned from those pros earlier.

YOUR INVISIBLE TEACHERS   224

Approximately 300 titles from literature are the basis for the activities in *Paragraphs for High School: A Sentence-Composing Approach*. Included are model sentences and paragraphs from hundreds of authors—your silent mentors, your invisible teachers. Here they all are, all of whom work hard at their craft to make reading easy for their readers.

WITH GRATITUDE

Thanks, deep and wide, to the hundreds of authors within—your mentors in this apprenticeship in sentence composing for better paragraphs—for modeling good writing and showing you the way to better writing through imitation to creation.

THE SENTENCE–PARAGRAPH LINK

The foundation of this worktext is a profound observation about good writing: it is the "add-ons" that differentiate the writing of authors from the writing of students. In other words, good writing is a process of addition. Good writers say more. State-mandated and other writing tests confirm this characteristic of good writing: the biggest reason students perform poorly on such tests is failure to elaborate. Contrast these two paragraphs to see the dramatic difference the underlined add-ons make:

BASIC PARAGRAPH

A twelve-year-old boy sat up in bed. There was a sound coming from outside. It was a huge, heavy rush. It was coming from directly above the house. The boy swung his legs off the bed. The yard was otherworldly. The boy stood on the lawn.

ELABORATE PARAGRAPH

In the predawn darkness, in the back bedroom of a small house in Torrance, California, a twelve-year-old boy sat up in bed, listening. There was a sound coming from outside, growing ever louder. It was a huge, heavy rush, suggesting immensity, a great parting of air. It was coming from directly above the house. The boy swung his legs off the bed, raced down the stairs, slapped open the back door, and loped onto the grass. The yard was otherworldly, smothered in unnatural darkness, shivering with sound. The boy stood on the lawn, head thrown back, spellbound.

Laura Hillenbrand, *Unbroken*

The underlined parts are the result of the author's use of sentence-composing tools that add elaboration. Here's good news: you can own the same tools authors use to build sentences to add elaboration for their paragraphs.

The goal of *Paragraphs for High School: A Sentence-Composing Approach* is to learn those sentence-composing tools and then use those tools through activities including imitating paragraphs, unscrambling paragraphs, building paragraphs, expanding paragraphs, creating paragraphs.

In the past, paragraphs were taught mainly as specimens for dissection, not as models for imitation. Instruction rarely went beyond "topic sentence" and "clincher sentence" and types of content (comparison, contrast, definition, narration, process, and so forth). Far too often, results were anemic paragraphs unlike paragraphs of good writers.

Paragraphs for High School: A Sentence-Composing Approach teaches, instead, imitation of real paragraphs, worthy models by authors. With this approach, and only a single paragraph as a manageable model, and with frequent imitation through varied activities, you can succeed, often astonishingly, in writing paragraphs like those of authors.

Words are the raw materials of writing. All sentences are made up of words. All paragraphs are made up of sentences. What makes the writing of good writers different from the writing of poor writers? The answer is how those words, sentences, and paragraphs are shaped and styled.

In this worktext, *Paragraphs for High School: A Sentence-Composing Approach*, you'll see how more than 300 authors shaped and styled their sentences and paragraphs, and, through the many activities sprung from those sentences and paragraphs, how you can similarly shape and style your own sentences and paragraphs. Those authors are your invisible teachers.

Through their sentences and their paragraphs, those hundreds of authors are ready to teach you the essential link between good sentences and good paragraphs.

If there is more important work than teaching,
I hope to learn about it before I die.

—Pat Conroy, *My Reading Life*

Learn everything you can from your teachers, visible and invisible, as they go about the important work of teaching you how to build better sentences and paragraphs.

BEST SENTENCES

Lists of "bests" recommend what to buy, see, read, view, hear, wear, visit, and so forth. What about writing? A helpful way to improve your writing is to study the best practices of good writers, namely, authors whose writing is widely read and appreciated.

This book focuses on those best practices, zooming in on the basic component of writing: the sentence. Learning how authors write "best sentences" for paragraphs is the purpose of this book, with activities and assignments to help you build better sentences, and, through those sentences, better paragraphs, and, through those paragraphs, better stories, essays, and reports.

What are "best sentences"? This section answers that question by demonstrating that they are sentences made up of three parts: subjects, predicates, and—the most important—tools.

THE MUST-HAVES: A SUBJECT AND A PREDICATE

Every sentence must have a subject. What is a subject? It's the topic that the writer makes a comment about in the rest of the sentence. Here is a list of topics. Some are single words, and others are phrases. They aren't subjects of sentences yet.

TOPICS

1. Willa
2. she
3. they
4. the young Italian
5. the wheels of wagons
6. the bare truth

7. cadavers and dead rats and frogs

8. Dad and some of his Air Force buddies

9. being a grandmother

10. to write down your reaction to important words and sentences you have read, and the questions they have raised in your mind

SUBJECTS AND PREDICATES

Below, the topic is now *the subject of a sentence* because the writer makes a comment about the topic. The comment is the other "must have" for a sentence, called the *predicate*. Notice that, like subjects, predicates can be any length: one word, or lots of words. Regardless of length, all predicates make a comment about their subject. In the list, subjects are bolded, and predicates are italicized.

1. **Willa** *sat by herself.*

2. **She** *forced smiles and held her tongue.*

3. **They** *came shuffling into the great concrete stadium.*

4. **The young Italian** *came along the sidewalk and walked quickly away into the darkness.*

5. **The wheels of wagons** *screeched.*

6. **The bare truth** *is you will only be an interesting artist the rest of your life.*

7. **Cadavers and dead rats and frogs** *appeared.*

8. **Dad and some of his Air Force buddies** *were on a cliff of the canyon.*

9. **Being a grandmother** *transformed her mother.*

10. **To write down your reaction to important words and sentences you have read, and the questions they have raised in your mind,** *preserves those reactions and sharpens those questions.*

THE SHOULD-HAVES: TOOLS

Every sentence must have a subject and a predicate, but "best sentences," the kind that authors write, also have something more: tools that build better sentences.

A tool is a sentence part that can be removed from the sentence without destroying the grammar of the sentence, a sentence part that adds detail and style to the sentence, a sentence part that is found in the great majority of sentences by authors, a sentence part that can build your own sentences in better ways like the "best sentences" of authors. Such tools improve your writing—often dramatically.

Adding tools to your sentences is probably the quickest, easiest, and most effective way to add content, style, and maturity to almost everything you write. Since writing is made up of sentences, building better sentences through the tools dramatically enhances what you write.

Like electrical power tools, sentence-composing tools come in different shapes and sizes. In the sentence pairs below, the first is without tools; the second with tools. Notice the huge difference. Used well, tools create best sentences.

SUBJECTS, PREDICATES, AND TOOLS

1a. Willa sat by herself.

1b. Willa sat by herself, **her high-necked flower-print dress looking out of place among the Levi's, denim skirts, and pearl-button shirts**.

Stephen King, *After Sunset*

2a. She forced smiles and held her tongue.

2b. On her monthly visits, dressed in stone marten furs, diamonds, and spike heels, which constantly caught between loose floorboards, she forced smiles and held her tongue.

Maya Angelou, *The Heart of a Woman*

3a. They came shuffling into the great concrete stadium.

3b. Laughing and shoving restlessly, damp-palmed with excitement, they came shuffling into the great concrete stadium, **some stopping to go to rest-rooms, some buying popcorn, some taking free pamphlets from the uniformed attendants**.

Steve Allen, "The Public Hating"

4a. The young Italian came along the sidewalk and walked quickly away into the darkness.

4b. The young Italian, **who had called to her earlier in the evening** and **who was now apparently setting out on his own Sunday evening's adventures**, came along the sidewalk and walked quickly away into the darkness.

Sherwood Anderson, "Unlighted Lamps"

5a. The wheels of wagons screeched.

5b. The wheels of wagons, **delivering feed or wood**, screeched, **as though they hurt**.

Toni Morrison, *Beloved*

6a. The bare truth is you will only be an interesting artist the rest of your life.

6b. The bare truth is, **if you do not learn a few more rudiments of the profession**, you will only be an interesting artist the rest of your life, **not a great one**.

J. D. Salinger, "De Daumier-Smith's Blue Period"

7a. Cadavers and dead rats and frogs appeared.

7b. Disgustingly, cadavers and dead rats and frogs appeared, **hidden in his locker about three months earlier**.

Gary Paulsen, *The Time Hackers*

8a. Dad and some of his Air Force buddies were on a cliff of the canyon.

8b. Dad and some of his Air Force buddies were on a cliff of the canyon, **trying to work up the nerve to dive into the lake forty feet below, when Mom and a friend drove up.**

Jeanette Walls, *The Glass Castle*

9a. Being a grandmother transformed her mother.

9b. Being a grandmother transformed her mother, **bringing a happiness and an energy her daughter had never witnessed.**

Jhumpa Lahiri, *Unaccustomed Earth*

10a. To write down your reaction to important words and sentences you have read, and the questions they have raised in your mind, preserves those reactions and sharpens those questions.

10b. Without a doubt, to write down your reaction to important words and sentences you have read, and the questions they have raised in your mind, preserves those reactions and sharpens those questions, **making what you read indelibly impressed upon your mind.**

Mortimer Adler, "How to Mark a Book"

Every sentence must have a subject and a predicate, but "best sentences" also have tools, which are the kind of sentence parts authors use. The proof is in the sentence pairs above.

The first is a sentence with just a subject and a predicate. It has what every sentence must have: a subject and a predicate. The second is a better sentence because it adds tools. It has what almost all authors' sentences have: tools that build better sentences, the kind you'll learn, practice, and use throughout this worktext to write your sentences like those of authors.

To be correct, a sentence must have a subject and a predicate, but *to be good, a sentence usually must also have tools*. Why? Because although authors' sentences have the basics (subjects and predicates), most of the information and style within their sentences is a result not of the subject and predicate, but of the tools.

ACTIVITY 1

Identify each sentence part in the author's sentence:

S = subject	P = predicate	T = tool

> **Remember:** Subjects and predicates cannot be removed from a sentence without destroying it. Tools can be removed (although no one would want to because they add so much to sentences). Use the removability tests for categorizing each listed sentence part as subject, predicate, or tool: if it's not removable, it's either a subject or a predicate; if it is removable, it's a tool.

EXAMPLE

His black hair, which had been combed wet earlier in the day, was dry now and blowing.

J. D. Salinger, "The Laughing Man"

a. His black hair, (*subject—not removable*)

b. which had been combed wet earlier in the day, (*tool—removable*)

c. was dry now and blowing. (*predicate—not removable*)

1. Carrie looked up, her eyes dazed from the heat and the steady, pounding roar of the water from the shower.

Stephen King, *Carrie*

a. Carrie

b. looked up,

c. her eyes dazed from the heat and the steady, pounding roar of the water from the shower.

2. To the surprise of one and all, in the first days of the war fever, Stobrod enlisted in the army.

Charles Frazier, Cold Mountain

   a. To the surprise of one and all,

   b. in the first days of the war fever,

   c. Stobrod

   d. enlisted in the army.

3. As the contest for the State Legislature that would name his successor raged in Missouri, Senator Benton stood fast by his post in Washington, outspoken to the end in his condemnation of the views his constituents now embraced.

John F. Kennedy, Profiles in Courage

   a. As the contest for the State Legislature that would name his successor raged in Missouri,

   b. Senator Benton

   c. stood fast by his post in Washington,

   d. outspoken to the end in his condemnation of the views his constituents now embraced.

4. More than midway down the block, Janet Gordon, who had been one of Clara's best friends, came out to pick up the baby.

Edward P. Jones, Lost in the City

   a. More than midway down the block,

   b. Janet Gordon,

   c. who had been one of Clara's best friends,

   d. came out to pick up the baby.

5. Out of breath from running, we three stood, staggering, coughing.

Annie Dillard, An American Childhood

    a. Out of breath from running,

    b. we three

    c. stood,

    d. staggering,

    e. coughing.

6. The feeling of family, a rare and treasured sentiment, pervades and accounts for the inability of the people to leave *the barrio*, a place of closeness.

Robert Ramirez, "The Barrio"

    a. The feeling of family,

    b. a rare and treasured sentiment,

    c. pervades and accounts for the inability of the people to leave *the barrio*,

    d. a place of closeness.

7. To demonstrate sisterhood and brotherhood with the plants and animals, the old-time people made animal masks and costumes, transforming the human figures of the dancers into the animal beings they portrayed.

Leslie Marmon Silko, Yellow Woman and a Beauty of the Spirit

    a. To demonstrate sisterhood and brotherhood with the plants and animals,

    b. the old-time people

    c. made animal masks and costumes,

    d. transforming the human figures of the dancers into the animal beings they portrayed.

8. The trip to the hospital was a nightmare, all three children crying, Cheri chain-smoking, his head ringing with bourbon and fatigue.

   Annie Proulx, "The Wamsutter Wolf"

   a. The trip to the hospital

   b. was a nightmare,

   c. all three children crying,

   d. Cheri chain-smoking,

   e. his head ringing with bourbon and fatigue.

9. On a bus trip to London from Oxford University, a young man, obviously fresh from a pub, spotted me and went down on his knees in the aisle, breaking into his Irish tenor's rendition of "Maria" from *West Side Story*.

   Judith Ortiz Cofer, "The Myth of the Latin Woman"

   a. On a bus trip to London from Oxford University,

   b. a young man,

   c. obviously fresh from a pub,

   d. spotted me and went down on his knees in the aisle,

   e. breaking into his Irish tenor's rendition of "Maria" from *West Side Story*.

10. Once, at the Library of Congress in Washington, I was shown the contents of Lincoln's pockets on the night that he was shot at Ford's Theater, a Confederate bank note, perhaps acquired during the President's recent excursion to the fallen capital of Richmond, and a pocket knife.

    Gore Vidal, "Lincoln Up Close"

a. Once,

b. at the Library of Congress in Washington,

c. I

d. was shown the contents of Lincoln's pockets on the night that he was shot at Ford's Theater,

e. a Confederate bank note,

f. perhaps acquired during the President's recent excursion to the fallen capital of Richmond,

g. and a pocket knife.

ACTIVITY 2

Add a tool at each caret mark (^). The first words of the tools are provided. The last five sentences illustrate that good writers sometimes use more than one tool to tell their readers more within the sentence. *Important:* Tools are sentence parts, not sentences. Don't add another sentence, just a sentence part.

EXAMPLE

Incomplete Sentence: In the other narrow bed, his brother went on sleeping, undisturbed by ^ .

Sample Addition: In the other narrow bed, his brother went on sleeping, <u>undisturbed by the loud snoring of his brother from the other twin bed.</u>

Original: In the other narrow bed, his brother went on sleeping, <u>undisturbed by the alarm clock's rusty ring.</u>

Gina Berriault, "The Stone Boy"

1. When ^ , each of the ladies had a chocolate moustache on her upper lip.

> Ray Bradbury, "The Whole Town's Sleeping"

2. To ^ , she would have to practice every day.

> Eleanor Coerr, *Sadako and the Thousand Paper Cranes*

3. My brother Buckley went on a day-trip to the Museum of Natural History in New York, where ^ .

> Alice Sebold, *The Lovely Bones*

4. At ^ , a number of men had gathered into a tight, jostling ring around a very pretty, very young woman who was talking at what must have been the top of her lungs.

> Michael Chabon, *The Amazing Adventures of Kavalier & Clay*

5. My mother had always been stunning, but when ^ , she was as beautiful as anyone I had ever seen.

> Joyce Weatherford, *Heart of the Beast*

6. Rob settled down, his back ^ , trying ^ .

> John Christopher, *The Guardians*

7. Sara watched him as he walked, a small ^ , wearing ^ .

> Betsy Byars, *The Summer of the Swans*

8. Clad in ^ , he was seated upon a throne, which ^ .

> Antoine de Saint-Exupéry, *The Little Prince*

9. Very ^ , as if ^ , Miles looked up.

> Susan Patron, *The Higher Power of Lucky*

10. Across ^ , into ^ , into ^ , the boy followed the dog, whose ^ .

> William Armstrong, *Sounder*

USING TOOLS TO ENHANCE A PARAGRAPH

ASSIGNMENT

Improve the paragraph by adding tools to each of its sentences at each caret mark (^).

WRITING PROCESS

Researching: Review the subjects, predicates, and tools described earlier in this section.

Prewriting: Think of descriptive details that would add originality and impact to this basic paragraph:

In the cafeteria Shaunte and Ramone accidentally-on-purpose sat at the same table, near a ^ but away from ^ . (2) They were in the same biology class, but had never met. (3) Once when ^ , Ramone really caught her attention because ^ . (4) With ^ , Shaunte, her voice ^ , asked Ramone a question, something about ^ . (5) Surprised that ^ , Ramone smiled and, struggling to ^ , came up with what he hoped was a neat answer, an answer that ^ . (6) The two of them, with ^ , with ^ and with ^ , made small talk while ^ . (7) When ^ , Shaunte said she had to leave, but Ramone, trying to ^ , hoping that ^ , persuaded her to stay, ignoring ^ . (8) After ^ , delighted that ^ , she sat down again, hoping ^ .

Drafting: Draft a paragraph with tools inserted at each caret. Within your paragraph, use a variety of types and lengths of tools. To get ideas, reread examples of tools from earlier in this section.

Peer responding and revising: Exchange your draft with other students in your class for suggestions to improve your paragraph, and give them suggestions, too. Then revise several times until your paragraph is finished.

Creating a title: Create a memorable title that previews the story in your paragraph. Don't make it predictable ("A Scary Night"). Instead make it understandable only after the reader finishes reading ("Demented Darkness").

In the next section "Show Me How: Sentences," you'll see lots of authors' examples of "best sentences," which use subjects, predicates—*and especially tools.* You'll learn and practice how to write sentences built like theirs to write "best sentences" of your own.

SHOW ME HOW: SENTENCES

"Show me how to do it." You've probably said that many times, asking somebody to demonstrate something you wanted to learn: how to swing a bat, how to style your hair, how to drive a car, how to make a recipe, how to solve a math problem—how to do just about anything.

The same is true with writing. Throughout this worktext, you'll watch writers demonstrate their craft in their sentences and paragraphs, imitate how they do it, and then do it yourself.

Since writing is made up of sentences, a good place to start is learning how authors write sentences and imitating how they do it.

ACTIVITY 1

In each pair, identify the sentence divided into parts that make sense.

1a. I was stiff, sore, and / exhausted, barely / grateful to / be alive.

1b. I was stiff, sore, / and exhausted, / barely grateful / to be alive.

Yann Martel, *Life of Pi*

2a. Clare snored, quiet / animal / snores that felt like bulldozers running / through my head.

2b. Clare snored, / quiet animal snores / that felt like bulldozers / running through my head.

Audrey Niffenegger, *The Time Traveler's Wife*

3a. Contrary to / popular / impressions, leprosy is not highly / contagious.

3b. Contrary / to popular impressions, / leprosy is not / highly contagious.

Norman Cousins, *Anatomy of an Illness*

4a. On a Saturday afternoon in July 1938, / a half-starved teenager / wandered into a bus station / in Columbus, Ohio, / appearing confused and disoriented.

4b. On a Saturday / afternoon in July 1938, a half-starved teenager / wandered into a / bus station in Columbus, / Ohio, appearing confused and disoriented.

Laura Hillenbrand, *Seabiscuit*

5a. Alma felt / as if she should make a wish, / like blowing out candles, / like seeing the first star / in the sky.

5b. Alma felt as / if she should make a wish, like blowing / out candles, like seeing the first / star in / the sky.

Julia Alvarez, *Saving the World*

6a. Henry arrived home, / bringing the dog food and other supplies / that Edgar had requested / and several cans / of paint and brushes.

6b. Henry arrived / home, bringing the dog food and other / supplies that Edgar had requested and several / cans of / paint and brushes.

David Wroblewski, *Edgar Sawtelle*

7a. As he drifted to sleep, out of the surrounding / silence and darkness came the quiet / ringing of a distant / church / bell, thin, faint, but clear.

7b. As he drifted to sleep, / out of the surrounding silence and darkness / came the quiet ringing / of a distant church bell, / thin, faint, but clear.

Richard Wright, *Native Son*

8a. Emilio stood in the hospital morgue / to identify his wife and child, / a doctor of forensic medicine lifting off a sheet and exposing their faces, / their eyes closed, / their expressions surprisingly serene.

8b. Emilio stood in the hospital / morgue to identify his wife and child, a doctor of forensic / medicine lifting off a sheet and exposing their faces, their eyes / closed, their expressions surprisingly / serene.

Oscar Hijuelos, The Fourteen Sisters of Emilio Montez O'Brien

9a. Writing his former / girlfriend, he invented stories of beach parties, sailing trips to Bermuda, art openings, a planned summer / trip to Europe, the purchase of a golden / retriever, a fishing trip to the Gulf of Mexico, a spiritual retreat to Mepkin Abbey, and a hundred other remarkable / events that never happened because his / letters were pure fiction.

9b. Writing his former girlfriend, / he invented stories of beach parties, sailing trips to Bermuda, art openings, a planned summer trip to Europe, the purchase of a golden retriever, a fishing trip to the Gulf of Mexico, a spiritual retreat to Mepkin Abbey, / and a hundred other remarkable events / that never happened / because his letters / were pure fiction.

Pat Conroy, South of Broad

10a. The baseball struck my mother's left temple, / spinning her so quickly that one of her high heels broke / and she fell forward, facing the stands, / her knees splaying apart, / her face hitting the ground first / because her hands never moved from her sides, / killing her before she touched the ground.

10b. The baseball struck my mother's / left temple, spinning her so / quickly that one of her high / heels broke / and she fell forward, facing the stands, her knees splaying apart, her / face hitting the ground / first because her hands never moved from her sides, killing her before she touched the ground.

John Irving, A Prayer for Owen Meany

ACTIVITY 2

Underneath the author's sentence are three sentences. Which two imitate the author's sentence?

1. **Author's Sentence:** Inside his office, he napped for an hour, snoring so loudly that his secretary finally had to close his door.

   John Grisham, *The Brethren*

   a. At her desk, she studied for the test, concentrating so intensely that her roommate eventually had to leave the room.

   b. The children by the river played contentedly, making odd dolls dressed in colorful leaves from the tree above them.

   c. Across the field, she ran like a gazelle, moving so gracefully that her coach ultimately decided to choose her.

2. **Author's Sentence:** I like Sherlock Holmes, but I do not like Sir Arthur Conan Doyle, who was the author of the Sherlock Holmes stories.

   Mark Haddon, *The Curious Incident of the Dog in the Night-Time*

   a. I eat ice cream bars, but I do not eat nutritious energy snacks, which are the foundation for various diet strategies.

   b. I read Stephen King, yet I do not read Edgar Allan Poe, who is the originator of the horror genre.

   c. I am going to summer camp, and I am very happy with the activities there because they teach me new skills.

3. **Author's Sentence:** It was a queer, sultry summer, the summer that they electrocuted the Rosenbergs, and I didn't know what I was doing in New York.

   Sylvia Plath, *The Bell Jar*

a. Mario owned a computer featuring the latest processor, with a sleek housing that contained all the software, and an operating system that beat all the competition.

b. There was a loud, explosive noise, a noise when he pressed the foot pedal, and he didn't know why the engine was stopping at the light.

c. The juggler was a very strange, quirky contestant, the one that they eliminated from competition, but they did explain why they were disapproving of the juggler's performance.

4. **Author's Sentence:** Threading his way through the Ninsei crowds, he could smell his own stale sweat.

William Gibson, Neuromancer

a. Walking slowly through the departing crowd emphasized their disappointment with the outcome.

b. Tapping the rhythm to the complicated song, he could imagine his own original variation.

c. Dancing her part in the Broadway musical, she could picture her own rising star.

5. **Author's Sentence:** She flicked her magic wand casually at the dishes in the sink, which began to clean themselves, clinking gently in the background.

J. K. Rowling, Harry Potter and the Chamber of Secrets

a. Brennan tossed his muddy shirt suddenly at the children in the pool, who wanted to play around, laughing together at the silliness.

b. The fairy flapped her lovely wings quietly over the castle near the lake, which started to resemble a mirror, reflecting magically in the moonlight.

c. Kylie noticed a suspicious person in the news conference and wondered why he was there taking notes and asking questions.

6. **Author's Sentence:** Suddenly there was no air in his punctured space suit, but he had enough air in his lungs to move his right hand over and twist a knob at his left elbow, tightening the joint and sealing the leak.

Ray Bradbury, "Kaleidoscope"

    a. Later the day turned into something beautiful, and Louise had so enjoyed the garden that morning that she looked forward to returning for sunset to watch the lightning bugs play in the darkness and rekindle her childhood.

    b. Then there was little food in his undersupplied bachelor apartment, but Liam had enough food in his refrigerator to cook a last meal slowly and enjoy a cup of day-old coffee, imagining other times and tasting other food.

    c. Afterwards there was no time at the crowded celebration party, but Teagan had enough time in the morning to line up his family and take a photograph in the front yard, commemorating the day and documenting the event.

7. **Author's Sentence:** Rebecca watched a skeletal man on crutches shuffle through the emergency room, guided by some kind of aide, a round-faced young girl who kept an arm around his waist.

Anne Tyler, *Back When We Were Grownups*

    a. Nate noticed a formally dressed woman on high heels cross through the conference room, followed by some sort of reporter, a solemn-faced older man who fixed an eye on the woman's notes.

    b. Brooks saw a monarch butterfly with stripes hover over the butterfly bush, attracted by some kind of blossom, a fluffy-looking purplish bloom that signaled an attraction for the insect.

    c. Nobody could understand why Shea, a brilliant doctor who specialized in neurological surgery, decided to leave the practice and stop surgery after she returned from research at the disease center.

8. **Author's Sentence:** They recalled the chicken salad LeRoy brought to the Labor Day potluck picnic, which had been sitting in the rear window of his car for a few hours, and the waves of propulsive vomiting it caused.

Garrison Keillor, *Pontoon*

   a. No one had prepared them for the intensity of the storm, and for the danger that they were sailing into, the possibility of a tornado hitting the lake and the surrounding area.

   b. The students discussed the unreasonable demands Matilda brought to the student council monthly meeting, which had been festering in the back of her mind since the last meeting, and the outburst of unanticipated anger those demands caused.

   c. They noticed the outrageous, flamboyant costume Henry wore to the high school Halloween dance, which had been stored in the dank garage of his neighbor for a few years, and the jeers of cruel laughter it evoked.

9. **Author's Sentence:** Sarah, tears rolling down her cheeks, kissed Mack on the forehead, simply, and then held on to Nan, who again broke into sobs and moans.

William P. Young, *The Shack*

   a. Maria, afraid that she would be left behind, started to run after the other girls from the party, her shouts echoing around them, furious that they left without her.

   b. Kim, eyes darting throughout the room, found Jay's body in the corner, sadly, and frantically looked for Justin, who awkwardly stumbled around debris and casualties.

   c. Alfred, rain pounding across his back, protected Maura Kate from the deluge, gently, and then rushed over to the picnic table, which teemed unfortunately with food and insects.

10. Author's Sentence: In the mango grove, shade poured into his black eyes when he played as a boy, when his mother sang, when the sacred offerings were made, when his father taught him, when the wise men talked.

Hermann Hesse, Siddhartha

a. In the school room, colors danced across the blank walls as he fantasized in his imagination, as the teacher smiled, as the quirky music was played, as his friend tickled him, as the other children giggled.

b. On the playing field, energy surged throughout his agile body, when he kicked like a pro, when his coach applauded, when the ritual exercises were completed, when his teammates applauded him, when the loyal fans cheered.

c. Under the large tree where he had played as a child he often thought about the people he would no longer see, the places he would no longer go, the times that were no more, remembering the past warmly and with longing.

ACTIVITY 3

Match the imitation with the model it imitates.

Model Sentences	Imitations
1. When we held Owen Meany above our heads, when we passed him back and forth so effortlessly, we believed that Owen was weightless. John Irving, *A Prayer for Owen Meany*	**a.** The twin babies curled back to back in their crib, poking out with tiny fingers to explore outside the crib and blanket and reassure each other of safe surroundings.

2. The teacher chose an escort for Clarence, a small, wiry boy with a crew cut just growing out that resembled an untended garden.

Tracy Kidder, *Among Schoolchildren*

b. After I heard the song on the radio, after I listened day and night so faithfully, I thought that the song was wonderful.

3. The two apes lay head to head on their blankets, reaching up with lazy hands to examine each other's faces and chests and rid each other of imaginary bugs.

Sara Gruen, *Ape House*

c. There was a situation that was unfortunately turning out as an academic disgrace, a premeditated unbroken line of cheating occurrences that determined the final outcome of expulsion.

4. It was a Sunday that was gloriously living up to its pagan name, a bold rebel burst of warm weather that announced the impending vanquishing of winter.

Yann Martel, *Beatrice and Virgil*

d. The best thrill for the audience was the appearance of the striped Bengal tiger who started the show, Lightning Streak, the amazing tiger from the circus in South Africa.

5. The great surprise of the crowd was the presence of the frail-boned boy who led the cheerleaders, Trevor Poe, the first male cheerleader in the history of my state.

Pat Conroy, *South of Broad*

e. The florist selected an assortment of flowers, a vivid, bright arrangement with a stargazer lily popping out that spotlighted a gorgeous presentation.

ACTIVITY 4

Unscramble and write out the sentence parts to imitate the model sentence. Then write a sentence of your own that imitates the sentence parts of the model.

EXAMPLE

Model Sentence: She hit the ground running, her arms and legs pumping.

Sara Gruen, *Water for Elephants*

Scrambled Sentence Parts:

a. her fingers and nails picking

b. started the scab bleeding

c. Ellie

Unscrambled Imitation: Ellie started the scab bleeding, her fingers and nails picking.

Sample Student Imitation: Mom started the grass soaking, her hose and sprinkler working.

---

1. In her wallet she still carried a picture of her husband, a clean-shaven boy in his twenties, the hair parted on one side.

Jhumpa Lahiri, *Unaccustomed Earth*

1a. a constant reminder of his marriage

1b. he always stored a suit of white linen

1c. in his closet

1d. a dried flower pinned to one lapel

2. He hiked on along the ridge with his thumb hooked in the shoulder strap of the rifle, his hat pushed back on his head.

Cormac McCarthy, No Country for Old Men

    2a. with her voice subdued

    2b. Jasmine talked on about the party

    2c. her smile flickering on her face

    2d. by the surrounding sounds of the others

3. Mom was wearing a white bathing suit that showed off her figure and her skin, which was dark from the Arizona sun.

Jeanette Walls, The Glass Castle

    3a. by the mustard

    3b. Rafael was eating a messy hot dog

    3c. which was stained

    3d. that dribbled off his lips and his chin

4. Grabbing the weapon from the limp fingers, he sprung to his feet and began firing wildly in the general direction of the running man, who stopped to fire back.

Robert Ludlum, The Prometheus Deception

    4a. which began to make sense

    4b. Irene jumped to a conclusion

    4c. but then started thinking hard

    4d. pondering four choices on the multiple-choice question

    4e. about the two other choices

5. He balanced the tree branch in his hand for a moment, and then threw it with blinding speed, shattering it against another huge tree, which shook and trembled at the blow.

Stephenie Meyer, *Twilight*

> **5a.** he calculated the complicated formula in his head with no problem
>
> **5b.** which faded then disappeared beside his solution
>
> **5c.** checking it against other incorrect answers
>
> **5d.** and then recorded it with total accuracy

ACTIVITY 5

Study the model and a sample imitation, and then write your own imitation.

MODELS AND SAMPLE IMITATIONS

1. The poplar trees lined the redbrick driveway, which led to a pair of wrought-iron gates.

    Khaled Hosseini, *The Kite Runner*

    Sample: The curious toddler touched the stuffed animal, which felt like a blanket of soft furry velvet.

2. McTeague remembered his mother, who, with the help of the Chinaman, cooked for forty miners.

    Frank Norris, *McTeague*

    Sample: Frankie watched the pitcher, who, with the concentration of a surgeon, unleashed his best fast ball.

3. This boy was an ingenious liar, a lonely boy with a boundless desire to ingratiate himself.

Marilynne Robinson, *Housekeeping*

Sample: That dog was a dangerous pet, a vicious dog with a distinct tendency to bite anyone.

4. He lived alone, a gaunt, stooped figure who wore a heavy black overcoat and a misshapen fedora on those rare occasions when he left his apartment.

Barack Obama, *Dreams from My Father*

Sample: She worked hard, a petite, pretty girl who wanted a successful lucrative career and a perfect husband in her cute apartment when she came home.

5. After the clerk stamped the envelope and threw it into a sorting bin, I sat down, glum, and disheartened.

Yann Martel, *Life of Pi*

Sample: When the others heard the call and answered it with a shrill scream, I felt alone, bereft, and abandoned.

IMITATING SENTENCES WITHIN A PARAGRAPH

ASSIGNMENT

For a page in a Harry Potter story, write a paragraph (ten to fifteen sentences) as part of an incident that appears in any of the Harry Potter novels or movies.

WRITING PROCESS

Researching: Reread or review an incident from any of the Harry Potter novels or movies.

Prewriting: List details of that incident, including the names of people, places, or objects.

Drafting: Draft a paragraph telling part of the incident, pretending you are J. K. Rowling, the author of the Harry Potter novels.

Refining and revising: Choose three of the model sentences below by J. K. Rowling to imitate within your paragraph.

MODEL SENTENCES BY J. K. ROWLING

From *Harry Potter and the Sorcerer's Stone:*
Slowly, very slowly, the snake raised its head until its eyes were on a level with Harry's.

From *Harry Potter and the Chamber of Secrets:*
The room was dingy and windowless, lit by a single oil lamp dangling from the low ceiling.

From *Harry Potter and the Prisoner of Azkaban:*
A voice came suddenly out of the shadows, a soft, misty sort of voice.

From *Harry Potter and the Goblet of Fire:*
Bloodthirsty and brutal, the giants brought themselves to the point of extinction by warring amongst themselves during the last century.

From *Harry Potter and the Order of the Phoenix:*
Standing still and quiet in the gloom, the creatures looked eerie and sinister.

From *Harry Potter and the Half-Blood Prince:*
Stupefied, painted gold, stuffed into a miniature tutu and with small wings glued to its back, it glowered down at them all, the ugliest angel Harry had ever seen, with a large bald head like a potato and rather hairy feet.

From *Harry Potter and the Deathly Hallows:*
He was also sure that ghouls were generally rather slimy and bald, rather than distinctly hairy and covered in angry purple blisters.

Peer responding: Exchange your draft with other students in your class for suggestions to improve your paragraph, and give them suggestions, too. Then revise several times until your paragraph is finished.

Creating a title: Create a memorable title and subtitle, with a colon between them. *Example:* "Hogwarts School: Beyond the Basics."

SENTENCE-COMPOSING TOOLS
FOR BETTER PARAGRAPHS

In the following activities, you'll study paragraphs containing sentence-composing tools for you to learn, practice, and use in your own paragraphs.

Sentence-composing tools improve paragraphs by adding sentence parts to sentences in paragraphs. Those tools help you achieve an important goal of good writing: elaboration. They tell your readers more.

A paragraph is a collection of sentences, so better sentences make better paragraphs. Building anything well requires tools, good tools, the kind used by expert craftspeople. In building better sentences and paragraphs in the craft of writing, the best tools are those used by authors, the expert craftspeople. Here you will learn, practice, and use some of their tools for building better sentences and, through those sentences, better paragraphs.

A good start to building better sentences is to use sentence-composing tools. Soon you'll learn, practice, and use three power tools for building better sentences.

You'll study how authors use those three power tools, plus other tools, and learn how you can also use them for your writing in and beyond high school.

First, though, see why they are power tools. Below are pairs of sentences. The first sentence lacks one of the power tools you'll be learning. The second sentence contains that tool.

THE IDENTIFIER TOOL

1a. The hangman was waiting beside his machine.

1b. The hangman, <u>a gray-haired convict in the white uniform of the prison,</u> was waiting beside his machine.

George Orwell, "A Hanging"

2a. Maria was a town character.

2b. Maria was a town character, <u>a fat middle-aged woman who lived with her old mother on the outskirts of town</u>.

Judith Ortiz Cofer, Silent Dancing

THE ELABORATOR TOOL

3a. Then both wheeled around the corner.

3b. Then both wheeled around the corner, <u>motors growling</u>, <u>headlights glaring</u>, <u>sirens howling</u>.

Robert Lipsyte, The Contender

4a. The dragon came crashing and blundering out of the underbrush.

4b. The dragon came crashing and blundering out of the underbrush, <u>its scales glowing a greenish copper color</u>, <u>its soot-caked nostrils venting smoke</u>.

Stephen King, The Eyes of the Dragon

THE DESCRIBER TOOL

5a. Towering stone pillars rose to support a ceiling lost in darkness.

5b. Towering stone pillars rose to support a ceiling lost in darkness, <u>casting long</u>, <u>black shadows through the odd</u>, <u>greenish gloom that filled the place</u>.

J. K. Rowling, Harry Potter and the Chamber of Secrets

6a. The fish tried to escape by swimming toward shore.

6b. <u>Pursued by killer whales that prey upon them when seals are not to be found</u>, the fish tried to escape by swimming toward shore.

Joseph Krumgold, Onion John

In each pair, the second sentence attracts you because it uses one of the three sentence-composing power tools. In the next sections you'll learn, practice, and use them in your own writing, one power tool at a time.

Learning the tools is easy, but here's a warning. Playing a musical instrument, improving your performance in athletics or the arts, doing just about anything requiring skill, you have to practice until the skill becomes natural. Once that happens, the skill is yours forever! This is also true with learning to write. You'll be doing a lot of practices to learn the tools, but it will be worth it when, suddenly, you've got it forever, confidently building better sentences, and, through them, better paragraphs.

THE IDENTIFIER

Good writers give readers information needed to understand their writing. Sometimes writers include in their sentences names of persons, places, objects, and other kinds of names that readers might not understand unless the writer identifies them. That's when an *appositive*, the identifying tool, comes in handy.

Look at these sentences to see how appositives improve sentences.

WITHOUT IDENTIFIERS

I came to philosophy as a last resort.

Ned came in and let the boarders out.

The dictionary had a picture of an aardvark.

WITH IDENTIFIERS

<u>A professional football player, print and television journalist, academic English teacher and world-traveler</u>, I came to philosophy as a last resort.

John McMurtry, "Kill 'Em! Crush 'Em! Eat 'Em Raw!"

Ned, <u>the lanky high-school student who cleaned the cages and fed the animals morning and evening</u>, came in and let the boarders out.

Sue Miller, *While I Was Gone*

The dictionary had a picture of an aardvark, <u>a long-tailed, long-eared, burrowing African mammal living off termites caught by sticking out its tongue as an anteater does for ants</u>.

Malcolm X and Alex Haley, *The Autobiography of Malcolm X*

> **Remember this:** Appositives are sentence parts that identify people, places, or things. Many appositives begin with one of these words: *a, an, the*.

ACTIVITY 1

Match the appositive with the sentence. Write out each sentence, underlining the appositive. Notice the three places appositives occur in a sentence: *opener, S-V split, closer*.

Sentences	Appositives
1. ^ , he reminded me of a baby bird. Tracy Chevalier, *The Girl with a Pearl Earring*	a. the year that showed us we could make our own destinies
2. The paper had a black spot on it, ^ . Shirley Jackson, "The Lottery"	b. a former college football player, six foot two and a swollen 245 pounds, with thick, meaty hands, every finger broken and bent
3. This was 1979, ^ . Roya Hakakian, *Journey from the Land of No*	c. a tan cow named Blind Tillie
4. One of them, ^ , was Cold Sassy's champion milk producer. Olive Ann Burns, *Cold Sassy Tree*	d. the black spot Mr. Summers had made the night before with the heavy pencil in the coal-company office
5. My father was an intimidating giant of a man, ^ . Perri Knize, *A Piano Odyssey*	e. a bald slight man

ACTIVITY 2

Combine two sentences into just one sentence. Make the underlined part an appositive to insert at the caret (^) in the first sentence. Notice how appositives use commas for the places where they can occur in a sentence: *opener, S-V split, closer*.

EXAMPLE

Opener Appositive:

^ , he could have been anywhere between forty and sixty. He was <u>a balding</u>, <u>smooth-faced man</u>.

Combined: <u>A balding</u>, <u>smooth-faced man</u>, he could have been anywhere between forty and sixty.

Harper Lee, To Kill a Mockingbird

S-V Split Appositive:

One of their dogs, ^ , had disappeared. That dog was <u>the best one</u>.

Combined: One of their dogs, <u>the best one</u>, had disappeared.

Fred Gibson, Old Yeller

Closer Appositive:

When the tyrannosaur roared, it was a terrifying sound, ^ . The sound was <u>a scream from some other world</u>.

Combined: When the tyrannosaur roared, it was a terrifying sound, <u>a scream from some other world</u>.

Michael Crichton, Jurassic Park

OPENER APPOSITIVES

1. ^ , he stepped off the porch and with heavy footsteps and a heavier heart started the hike back to the car. He was <u>a weary old man</u>.

    William P. Young, *The Shack*

2. ^ , Harriet was a moody, willful child. She was <u>the third child of eleven brothers and sisters</u>.

    Langston Hughes, "Road to Freedom"

3. ^ , the North Star would soon be visible and would point the way when the birds had all gone South. That star was <u>the guidepost of her ancestors</u>.

    Jean Craighead George, *Julie of the Wolves*

4. ^ , Tom Black has ridden nine horses to death in the rodeo arena, and at every performance the spectators expect him to kill another one. Tom was <u>a veteran bronc rider</u>.

    Hal Borland, *When the Legends Die*

5. ^ , I was put in a special seat in the first row by the window apart from the other children so that Sister Zoe could tutor me without disturbing them. I was <u>the only immigrant in my class</u>.

    Julia Alvarez, *How the Garcia Girls Lost Their Accents*

S-V SPLIT APPOSITIVES

6. The real estate agent, ^ , soon joined them. The agent was <u>an old man with a smiling, hypocritical face</u>.

    Willa Cather, "The Sculptor's Funeral"

7. Manuel, ^ , had been operated on. Manuel was <u>the herder who shot</u> <u>himself in the foot</u>.

Hal Borland, When the Legends Die

8. The coachman, ^ , saluted Sir Henry Baskerville, and in a few minutes we were flying swiftly down the broad, white road. The coachman was <u>a hard-faced, gnarled little fellow</u>.

Sir Arthur Conan Doyle, The Hound of the Baskervilles

9. Angel and Jose, ^ , cackled like hens when the medicine ball knocked him over like a ten pin. Angel and Jose were <u>the Puerto Rican boys</u>.

Robert Lipsyte, The Contender

10. After a minute, two of the creatures, ^ , moved hesitantly down the slope and stood looking at him curiously. The creatures were <u>a doe</u> <u>and her fawn</u>.

Alexander Key, The Forgotten Door

CLOSER APPOSITIVES

11. There they were in the schoolroom again, ^ . They were <u>the five</u> <u>boys and Lina and the teacher</u>.

Meindert DeJong, The Wheel on the School

12. Stephanie was pointing at a picture, ^ . The picture was <u>a big faded</u> <u>photograph in a frame by the mirror</u>.

Richard Peck, Those Summer Girls I Never Met

13. Paddy became friendly with a cow from a near-by field, ^ . The cow was <u>a big, fat, brown animal with sleepy eyes and an enormous tail</u> <u>that coiled about its hind legs like a rope</u>.

Christy Brown, My Left Foot

14. Harry sat down between Dudley and Uncle Vernon, ^ . His uncle was <u>a large beefy man with very little neck and a lot of mustache</u>.

J. K. Rowling, *Harry Potter and the Prisoner of Azkaban*

15. From every window blows an incense, ^ . The incense is <u>the all-pervasive blue and secret smell of summer storms and lightning</u>.

Ray Bradbury, *Dandelion Wine*

ACTIVITY 3

To practice creating appositives, substitute a new appositive for the existing underlined one.

EXAMPLE

Author's Appositive: <u>A short, round boy of seven</u>, he took little interest in troublesome things, preferring to remain on good terms with everyone.

Mildred D. Taylor, *Roll of Thunder, Hear My Cry*

Student's Appositive: <u>A cagey, careful politician with voters</u>, he took little interest in troublesome things, preferring to remain on good terms with everyone.

1. <u>A thoroughbred of the streets</u>, Jemmy acted on instinct.

Sid Fleischman, *The Whipping Boy*

2. Tobias, <u>the new member of our group</u>, was about a hundred feet above us, floating on a nice warm current of air.

K. A. Applegate, *Animorphs: The Underground*

3. Ulli Steltzer, <u>a photographer who then lived in Princeton and now lives in Vancouver</u>, remembers George as a boy.

    Kenneth Brower, *The Starship and the Canoe*

4. A moment later, Pepe heard the sound, <u>the faint far crash of horse's hoofs on gravel</u>.

    John Steinbeck, "Flight"

5. The country hailed Althea Gibson, <u>the rangy tennis player who was the first black female to win the U.S. Women's Singles</u>.

    Maya Angelou, *The Heart of a Woman*

ACTIVITY 4

Unscramble and write out the sentence parts to imitate the model sentence. Then write a sentence of your own that imitates all the sentence parts of the model, not just the appositives.

EXAMPLE

Model Sentence: The fifth traveler, <u>a withered old gentleman sitting next to the middle door across the aisle</u>, napped fitfully upon his cane.

Henry Sydnor Harrison, "Miss Hinch"

Scrambled Sentence Parts:

a. boomed loudly throughout the gym

b. a huge woofer delivering thunder to the sound of the band

c. the bass speaker

Unscrambled Imitation: The bass speaker, <u>a huge woofer delivering thunder to the sound of the band</u>, boomed loudly throughout the gym.

Sample Student Imitation: The smallest child, <u>a freckled little boy holding tight to the hand of his older brother</u>, waded merrily into the water.

---

1. He signaled to Jake, the middle brother, to take over the cash register.

Robert Lipsyte, *The Contender*

    1a. a four-wheel-drive model

    1b. he turned the car

    1c. to gain more traction

2. An elegant older man with swept-back white hair, Simpson was the world's leading authority on lizard taxonomy.

Michael Crichton, *Jurassic Park*

    2a. for words and numbers

    2b. an extremely gifted young man with a talent

    2c. Gerard was the school's highest scorer on the S.A.T.

3. I kept my eyes on my hands on the desk waiting for something to happen, an explosion, a battle cry, anything but the silence.

Rosa Guy, *The Friends*

    3a. anything but nothing

    3b. hoping for a fish to bite

    3c. a little one

    3d. they parked themselves on the edge of a bridge

    3e. a big one

4. The only son of a wealthy missionary couple, the Laughing Man was kidnapped in infancy by bandits.

J. D. Salinger, "The Laughing Man"

4a. the website was developed

4b. by students

4c. a smashing success

4d. in weeks

4e. from its first appearance

5. At that moment, a young man came into the bunk house, a thin man with a brown face, with brown eyes, and a head of tightly curled hair.

John Steinbeck, *Of Mice and Men*

5a. and a skill of absolutely perfect control

5b. in that event

5c. a young woman with an agile body

5d. a Canadian skier emerged with a gold medal

5e. with tremendous speed

ACTIVITY 5

Imitate each model sentence—all of it, not just the underlined appositive. Make your imitation so good that no one can tell which sentence is yours and which is the author's.

MODELS AND SAMPLE IMITATIONS

1. <u>A lifelong bachelor</u>, he had no family in America and so had become attached to ours.

    Jeffrey Eugenides, *Middlesex*

    Sample: <u>A flagrant flirt</u>, he had numerous girlfriends on campus and so had become envied by many.

2. The writer, <u>an old man with a white mustache</u>, had some difficulty getting into bed.

    Sherwood Anderson, *Winesburg, Ohio*

    Sample: The cartoonist, <u>a clever boy with a vivid imagination</u>, got some fun learning about comics.

3. On the south end of the garden, in the shadows of the loquat tree, was the servants' home, <u>a modest little mud hut where Hassan lived with his father</u>.

    Khaled Hosseini, *The Kite Runner*

    Sample: In the computer lab of the engineering building, in the third row from the front of the room, was a forgotten laptop, <u>a shiny sleek Macintosh that a student had brought to the class</u>.

4. He heard the sound he dreaded, <u>the hollow, rasping cough of a horse</u>.

    John Steinbeck, *The Red Pony*

    Sample: She smelled the fragrance she loved, <u>the sweet honeysuckle on the fence</u>.

5. The judge, <u>an old, bowlegged fellow in a pale blue sweater</u>, had stopped examining the animals and was reading over some notes he had taken on the back of a dirty envelope.

    Jessamyn West, "The Lesson"

Sample: The suspect, <u>an anxious,</u> <u>tattooed girl in a revealing tank</u> <u>top</u>, started tapping her foot and was chewing on some hair she had pulled out of a pony tail in the back of her messy hair.

ACTIVITY 6

Add an appositive at each caret mark (^). The words that the appositives identify are bolded. The last five sentences illustrate that good writers sometimes use more than one appositive to identify the same thing in different ways.

EXAMPLE

Incomplete Sentence: After a few weeks Mother managed to buy me **a new car**, a ^ .

Sample Appositive: After a few weeks Mother managed to buy me a new car, <u>a moderately priced two-door compact that had</u> <u>been used as a demonstrator by the car dealership</u>.

Original: After a few weeks Mother managed to buy me a new car, <u>a proper invalid chair this time that had a nice padded seat</u> <u>and rubber tires</u>.

Christy Brown, *My Left Foot*

1. **Mrs. Botkin**, a ^ , looked at her husband and started to say something.

Evan Connell, Jr. "The Condor and the Guests"

2. A ^, **Henry Wingo** seemed to fill up every room he entered with a superabundance of energy.

Pat Conroy, *The Prince of Tides*

3. Harry Herman offered to let Stretch sit in **his favorite chair**, a ^ .

   Robert Cormier, *Take Me Where the Good Times Are*

4. I used to have **a cat**, an ^ , who would jump through the open window by my bed in the middle of the night and land on my chest.

   Annie Dillard, *Pilgrim at Tinker Creek*

5. At work he was training **a new employee**, a ^ .

   John Steinbeck, *The Grapes of Wrath*

6. There was **Pepe**, the ^ , a ^ .

   John Steinbeck, "Flight"

7. **Buck** the dog stood and looked on, the ^ , the ^ .

   Jack London, *The Call of the Wild*

8. The **sun** was the blessing of the morning, the ^ , an ^ .

   John Knowles, *A Separate Peace*

9. He tried to remember **every little thing** so he could store it away for later, the ^ , the ^ , the ^ .

   Robert Lipsyte, *The Contender*

10. He heard **every little sound** of the gathering night, the ^ , the ^ , the ^ , and the ^ .

    John Steinbeck, *The Pearl*

BUILDING PARAGRAPHS

The writer of the paragraph below learned how to use the identifier tool by doing appositive activities like the ones in this section. His class was then given an assignment to write a paragraph to review an event in entertainment or sports. (Appositives are italicized.)

Radiohead Live: A Sonic, Techno Dazzler
by Tim Morzek
(*a student paper*)

(1) Radiohead is no stranger to breaking new ground, but with the release of their two new albums, *two highly experimental and electronic records*, many questions arose as to how they might perform the music live—*concerns that were quickly resolved at last night's concert*. (2) The venue was packed at the Gorge Amphitheatre, *a natural, outdoor music arena*, as many fans of Radiohead eagerly but restlessly awaited the appearance of the band. (3) Nearing dusk, Thom Yorke and the rest of his band took the stage amidst gales of applause and cheers. (4) The crowd's concern over whether or not these guys could pull off such strange and atmospheric music was quickly laid to rest as the band began with "Packed Like Sardines in a Crushed Box," *the first track off their newest album Amnesiac, a great kick-off for the album*. (5) At this point everyone realized that not only did Radiohead have the ability to perform these very experimental songs, *dazzlers that most bands couldn't even dream of attempting live because of the techno challenges*, but they were able to play them even better live than in a techno-rich recording studio. (6) As the sun began to set over the mountains in the distance, creating a very interesting mood, intensified by the very emotional moods of Radiohead's music, Thom began to play one of the band's most recognized and adored songs, "Paranoid Android," *a "Bohemian Rhapsody"-like epic song consisting of three original songs put together to form what is considered by some the quintessence of Radiohead's genius*. (7) Thom, pumping his fist during one of the more intense parts, his voice echoing off of the mountains and into the concertgoers' hearts, brought

the song together with his hauntingly beautiful vocals. (8) *The band's most creative and versatile member with a new show-stopper at every live concert*, Johnny Greenwood played one of his custom-wired guitars, giving the live version of the song the original sound for which that guitar has become known. (9) At the same time, Colin Greenwood, *Johnny's older brother*, stood between Thom and Johnny, playing the smooth yet odd bass line that really holds the song together. (10) Ed O'Brien, *the most "normal" of the band members*, was on the far left playing with his many pedals that give his guitar its unique sound. (11) All the while, Phil Selway, *the band's percussionist*, sat, sadly obscured by the others, yet heard clearly, holding the song to the proper pace and rhythm. (12) The entire concert was memorable, *a sonic, techno dazzler*.

USING APPOSITIVES TO BUILD A PARAGRAPH

For an article in your school's newspaper, write a one-paragraph review of an event in sports or entertainment.

WRITING PROCESS

Researching: Attend or recall the event.

Prewriting: List important terms associated with that event. Choose terms probably unfamiliar to your readers. For example, for the sport lacrosse, key terms are *attackman* and *midfielder*; for a movie, terms could include *computer generated images* (*CGI*) and *docudrama*.

Drafting: Draft a paragraph informing your readers about the event, using appositives to identify important terms. Use appositives in different places and lengths, and sometimes use more than one appositive within the same sentence.

Peer responding and revising: Exchange your draft with other students in your class for suggestions to improve your paragraph, and give them suggestions, too. Then revise several times until your paragraph is finished.

Creating a title: Create a memorable title and subtitle, with a colon between them. *Examples:* "CGI: Making Fake Real" or "Football: The Torture Sport."

THE ELABORATOR

For good writing, more is usually better. Elaborating is a way of telling your readers more information and details so they understand clearly and completely what you're writing about. An *absolute*, the elaborating tool, gives readers more.

Look at these sentences to see how absolutes improve sentences.

WITHOUT ELABORATORS

He lifted the truck in one fluid, powerful motion.

A teenager in a black tank top hoisted a toddler onto her shoulder.

Mattie drank most of what was left.

WITH ELABORATORS

The sweat popping off his skin like oil on water, he lifted the truck in one fluid, powerful motion.

Mildred D. Taylor, *Roll of Thunder, Hear My Cry*

A teenager in a black tank top, a greenish tattoo flowing across her broad back, hoisted a toddler onto her shoulder.

Barbara Kingsolver, *Animal Dreams*

Mattie drank most of what was left, the ice cubes sliding against her teeth with a click and a rattle.

Stephen King, *Bag of Bones*

Remember this: Absolutes are sentence parts that elaborate information. Every absolute could be a complete sentence if you added *was* or *were*. Here are the absolutes from above changed to sentences by adding *was* or *were*.

1. The sweat **was** popping off his skin like oil on water.

2. A greenish tattoo **was** flowing across her broad back.

3. The ice cubes **were** sliding against her teeth with a click and a rattle.

ACTIVITY 1

Match the absolute with the sentence. Write out each sentence, underlining the absolute. Notice the three places absolutes occur in a sentence: *opener*, *S-V split*, *closer*.

Sentences	Absolutes
1. He began scrambling up the wooden pegs nailed to the side of the tree, ^ . John Knowles, *A Separate Peace*	**a.** hands and limbs swollen with venom
2. ^ , my face and bare skin welted red. Keith Donohue, *The Stolen Child*	**b.** his heavy shoes making the snow crackle
3. A seared man, ^ , rose from the curb. Fritz Leiber, "A Bad Day for Sales"	**c.** his charred clothes fuming where the blast had blown out the fire
4. He paused at the intersection, ^ . Anne Tyler, *Saint Maybe*	**d.** his back muscles working like a panther's
5. The young man walked down the frozen land, ^ . James Michener, *Centennial*	**e.** the arches of his sneakers teetering on the curb

ACTIVITY 2

Combine two sentences into just one sentence. Make the underlined part an absolute to insert at the caret (^) in the first sentence. Notice how absolutes use commas for the places where they can occur in a sentence: *opener, S-V split, closer.*

EXAMPLES

Opener Absolute:

^ , I reeled around to face Boo Radley and his bloody fangs. <u>My shoulders</u> were <u>up</u>.

Combined: <u>My shoulders up</u>, I reeled around to face Boo Radley and his bloody fangs.

> Harper Lee, *To Kill a Mockingbird*

S-V Split Absolute:

A wild-eyed horse, ^ , trotted frantically through the mounds of men, tossing its head, whinnying in panic. <u>Its bridle</u> was <u>torn and dangling</u>.

Combined: A wild-eyed horse, <u>its bridle torn and dangling</u>, trotted frantically through the mounds of men, tossing its head, whinnying in panic.

> Lois Lowry, *The Giver*

Closer Appositive:

The baby slept, ^ . Its cheek was <u>sideways against her shoulder</u>.

Combined: The baby slept, <u>its cheek sideways against her shoulder</u>.

> John Steinbeck, *The Pearl*

OPENER ABSOLUTES

1. ^ , she stood in the middle of the courtyard. <u>Her knees</u> were <u>half-bent</u>.

   Roya Hakakian, Journey from the Land of No

2. ^ , my mother wandered by and stood in the doorway, listening intently. <u>A dust rag</u> was <u>in her hand</u>.

   Keith Donohue, The Stolen Child

3. ^ , the three of us strolled as casually as we could to the front yard. <u>Our respiration</u> was <u>normal</u>.

   Harper Lee, To Kill a Mockingbird

4. ^ , they saw, flat on the floor in front of them, a troll even larger than the one they had tackled out cold. <u>Their eyes</u> were <u>watering</u>.

   J. K. Rowling, Harry Potter and the Sorcerer's Stone

5. ^ , slowly rising from his hiding place, he took a step forward when suddenly the bush behind him seemed to explode. <u>His gun</u> was <u>still drawn</u>.

   William P. Young, The Shack

S-V SPLIT ABSOLUTES

6. The small dragon, ^ , wrapped its tail around the bedpost content-edly. <u>Its eyes</u> were <u>closed</u>.

   Christopher Paolini, Eragon

7. A windjammer, ^ , seemed to be passing along the starboard side. <u>Its sails</u> were <u>set</u>.

   Walter Lord, A Night to Remember

8. Two hard-faced men, ^ , stood watching him closely from the adjacent guard station. <u>Both</u> were <u>cradling submachine guns</u>.

    Robert Ludlum, *The Moscow Vector*

9. A thick scarf, ^ , was crossed over his chest. <u>Its ends</u> were <u>tucked into his coat</u>.

    Leslie Morris, "Three Shots for Charlie Beston"

10. Harry, ^ , watched Riddle stop between the high pillars and look up into the stone face of Slytherin, high above him in the half-darkness. <u>Fear</u> was <u>spreading up his numb legs</u>.

    J. K. Rowling, *Harry Potter and the Chamber of Secrets*

CLOSER ABSOLUTES

11. At the foot of one of the trees, the boy's father sat, ^ . <u>The lantern</u> was <u>still burning by his side</u>.

    William Armstrong, *Sounder*

12. For a moment we stood in silence, ^ . <u>Only the forest sounds</u> were <u>cracking the stillness</u>.

    Mildred D. Taylor, *Let the Circle Be Unbroken*

13. They were just outside the entrance to the hole, ^ . <u>Each one</u> was <u>crouching behind a tree with his gun loaded</u>.

    Roald Dahl, *Fantastic Mr. Fox*

14. The eyes were cold, ^ . <u>The skin around them</u> was <u>wrinkled and leathery as though from long staring into harsh sunlight and bleak winds</u>.

    John Christopher, *The Guardians*

15. He was wearing Boy Scout pants, and on the back of his head was a skullcap made from the crown of a man's felt hat, ^ . <u>The edge</u> was <u>turned up and cut into sharp points that were ornamented with brass.</u>

Murray Heyert, "The New Kid"

ACTIVITY 3

To practice creating absolutes, substitute a new absolute for the existing underlined one.

EXAMPLE

> *Author's Absolute:* He walked away from the street, <u>his shadow leading the way.</u>
>
> David Wroblewski, *Edgar Sawtelle*
>
> *Student's Absolute:* He walked away from the street, <u>his faithful dog behind him</u>.

---

1. <u>Pain shooting up my entire arm</u>, I lay panting on the edge of the pool and gingerly began to feel my wrist.

Theodore Taylor, *The Cay*

2. <u>The flies crawling endlessly on him</u>, Ben felt everything dropping away.

Robb White, *Deathwatch*

3. Gerard, <u>his elbows spread wide on the arms of his chair</u>, stretched his legs further under the table and looked at the fire.

Elizabeth Bowen, "Foothold"

4. Stacey stopped, <u>a worried look on his face</u>.

Mildred D. Taylor, Song of the Trees

5. Dawn was starting to break over the mountain peaks, <u>the colors of early morning sunrise beginning to identify themselves against the ashy gray of the escaping night</u>.

William P. Young, The Shack

ACTIVITY 4

Unscramble and write out the sentence parts to imitate the model sentence. Then write a sentence of your own that imitates all the sentence parts of the model, not just the absolutes.

EXAMPLE

Model Sentence: He snapped awake and scrambled clumsily to his feet, <u>his muscles sore and stiff from lying on the floor</u>.

William P. Young, The Shack

Scrambled Sentence Parts:

a. and stretched easily into the pose

b. and adept from training for the dance

c. she reached down

d. her body limber

Unscrambled Imitation: She reached down and stretched easily into the pose, <u>her body limber and adept from training for the dance</u>.

Sample Student Imitation: The car swerved right and entered smoothly into the curve, <u>its driver sure and skillful about turning at that angle</u>.

----

1. Hunched, her knees bent, she stood in the middle of the courtyard.

    Robert Lipsyte, *The Contender*

    1a. her breath gasping

    1b. she hid in the corner of the closet

    1c. frightened

2. His heart pounding, Bod walked out into the world.

    Neil Gaiman, *The Graveyard Book*

    2a. over to the coach

    2b. Jay limped

    2c. his feet sore

3. They hung up their rifles and changed their ways, each peaceably fading into history after shaking things up.

    Aron Ralston, *Between a Rock and a Hard Place*

    3a. and cooked their burgers

    3b. each carefully looking at the meat

    3c. they put on their aprons

    3d. after turning patties over

4. Only the orange power light at the base of the freezer was visible, its bulb winking and flickering.

David Wroblewski, *Edgar Sawtelle*

   4a. its shriek wailing and upsetting

   4b. in the basement of the house

   4c. only the smoke detector alarm

   4d. was audible

5. Mr. Murray, who had been sitting, his elbows on his knees, rose.

Madeleine L'Engle, *A Wrinkle in Time*

   5a. who had been watching

   5b. the referee

   5c. his whistle at his mouth

   5d. froze

ACTIVITY 5

Imitate each model sentence—all of it, not just the underlined absolute. Make your imitation so good that no one can tell which sentence is yours and which is the author's.

MODELS AND SAMPLE IMITATIONS

1. On the floor, <u>its head resting on one of the man's feet</u>, lay an old white English bull terrier.

Sheila Burnford, *The Incredible Journey*

Sample: In the closet, <u>its handle leaning on one of the abandoned suitcases</u>, stood a torn battered used umbrella.

2. Across the expanse of stakes and seedlings, the stray dog stood, eating greedily and watching Edgar, <u>its chest silver in the moonlight</u>.

   David Wroblewski, *Edgar Sawtelle*

   Sample: On the table of supplies and materials, the paint brush waited, lying quietly and tempting Sam, <u>its bristles clean in the sunlight</u>.

3. The nationalist on the stepladder, <u>his quick hands slashing through the air</u>, was whipping his growing audience out of its morning listlessness.

   Robert Lipsyte, *The Contender*

   Sample: The singer on the stage, <u>his heavy feet stomping on the boards</u>, was leading his young fans into a throbbing frenzy.

4. The scorpion hoisted herself out of the matchbox with great rapidity, <u>her babies clinging on desperately</u>, and scuttled onto the back of Larry's hand.

   Gerald Durrell, "The World in a Wall"

   Sample: The song insinuated itself into his memory with subtle strength, <u>its words holding on quietly</u>, and emerged into his consciousness at every sunset.

5. Harry saw that what had hold of him was marching on six immensely long, hairy legs, <u>the front two clutching him tightly below a pair of shining black pincers</u>.

   J. K. Rowling, *Harry Potter and the Chamber of Secrets*

   Sample: Dan thought that what had defeated him was thinking about many unlikely unsolvable problems, <u>the first one waking him insistently from a dream of dismal unfortunate failure</u>.

ACTIVITY 6

Add an absolute at each caret mark (^). The last five sentences illustrate that good writers sometimes use more than one absolute to elaborate the same situation in different ways.

EXAMPLE

Incomplete Sentence: By and by, we began to sing, the two of us ^ .

Sample Absolute: By and by, we began to sing, <u>the two of us blending in harmony.</u>

Original: By and by, we began to sing, <u>the two of us singing different songs simultaneously.</u>

Truman Capote, "A Christmas Memory"

---

1. His ^ , the shamefaced Taran hurried from the cottage and found Coll near the vegetable garden.

Lloyd Alexander, *The Book of Three*

2. Their ^ , he continued to work with the leaf, pulling off half-inch-wide strips and laying them in a pile.

Robb White, *Deathwatch*

3. A large car, its ^ , sped through the intersection against the red light.

Frank W. Dixon, *The Secret of the Old Mill*

4. She sat down, her ^ .

Robert Lipsyte, *The Contender*

5. On impulse, he went in, bought a bag of gumdrops, and went on up the street, his ^ .

   Hal Borland, *When the Legends Die*

6. Sitting alone in the dark, his ^ , some ^ , he started crying.

   Gary Paulsen, *Hatchet*

7. Exhausted, stomach ^ , mind ^ , Harry fell into an uneasy sleep.

   J. K. Rowling, *Harry Potter and the Chamber of Secrets*

8. The creatures, some ^ , others ^ , were all watching him intently.

   Roald Dahl, *James and the Giant Peach*

9. The whole surface of the wall was an intricate map of cracks, some ^ , others ^ .

   Gerald Durrell, "The World in a Wall"

10. I was alone and orphaned, in the middle of the Pacific Ocean, hanging on to an oar, ^ , ^ , ^ .

    Yann Martel, *Life of Pi*

USING ABSOLUTES TO BUILD A PARAGRAPH

Compose a paragraph for an Internet or paper newspaper telling in detail what happened in an event for readers who were not there.

WRITING PROCESS

Researching: Locate and paste into your document a picture of the event, preferably one with lots of action. Pretend you are a reporter writing what happened in the picture.

Prewriting: Study the picture and then list absolute phrases to describe specific details to include in your report.

Drafting: Draft a paragraph telling your readers the story in the picture. Since you are writing about an event that happened in the past, use past tense (*shouted, ran*) not present tense (*shouts, runs*). Within your paragraph, use absolutes in different places and lengths, and sometimes use more than one absolute within the same sentence.

Peer responding and revising: Exchange your draft with other students in your class for suggestions to improve your paragraph, and give them suggestions, too. Then revise several times until your paragraph is finished.

Creating a title: Create a memorable title that previews the story in your paragraph. Don't make it predictable ("The Winning Touchdown"). Instead make it understandable only after the reader finishes reading ("A White-Knuckle Finish").

BUILDING PARAGRAPHS

You've learned and practiced a sentence-composing tool for identifying (*the appositive*), and a tool for elaborating (*the absolute*). Now put those two tools to work to help build an opening paragraph for a story.

Pretend you are one of the authors below who has written the first sentence of a story that will take 300 pages to finish. Choose one of their sentences as the first sentence in a paragraph that will begin that 300-page story.

AUTHORS' SENTENCES

1. A beautiful animal, it lay in the position of a marble lion, its head toward a man sitting on an upturned bucket outside the cage.

    Frank Bonham, *Chief*

2. In the far corner, the man was still asleep, snoring slightly on the intaking breath, his head back against the wall.

Ernest Hemingway, "The Undefeated"

3. Harry twisted his body around and saw a grindylow, a small, horned water demon, poking out of the weed, its long fingers clutched tightly around Harry's leg, its pointed fangs bared.

J. K. Rowling, *Harry Potter and the Goblet of Fire*

4. Downstairs, she saw the girls sleeping where she'd left them, but back to back now, each wrapped tight in blankets, breathing into their pillows.

Toni Morrison, *Beloved*

5. The condemned man's hands were behind his back, the wrists bound with a cord.

Ambrose Bierce, "An Occurrence at Owl Creek Bridge"

6. They stood in the dead city, a heap of boys, their hiking lunches half devoured, daring each other in shrieky whispers.

Ray Bradbury, *The Martian Chronicles*

7. One of the boys, a pimply galoot with a silver cross dangling from his neck on a chain, had a baseball bat in a homemade sling on his back.

Stephen King, *Hearts in Atlantis*

8. Standing on the road was the man from the night before, the man in the yellow suit, his black hat on his head.

Natalie Babbitt, *Tuck Everlasting*

9. There it lay, this small oblong sea-green jellyfish thing, at the bottom of the jar, quite peaceful, but pulsing gently, the whole of it moving in and out ever so slightly, as though it were breathing.

    Roald Dahl, *The BFG*

10. The market, a large open square with wooden houses on two sides, some containing first-floor shops, was crowded with various carts laden with grains, vegetables, wood, hides, and whatnot.

    Bernard Malamud, *The Fixer*

Make up the rest of the paragraph, but somewhere in it use these sentence-composing tools:

*   appositives and absolutes in various lengths (*short, medium, long*)

*   appositives and absolutes in different places within the sentence (*opener, S-V split, closer*)

*   multiple appositives or absolutes within the same sentence

*   combination of appositives and absolutes within the same sentence

Important: You are just barely beginning a story, not writing a complete story, which would require 300 pages from start to finish. Zoom in on just one detail in your first paragraph of that story—an object, a place, a mood, an event, a person—some detail triggered by what's in the author's sentence you chose from this list.

SAMPLE PAPER

Before drafting your own paragraph, study the appositives (*italicized*) and absolutes (underlined) to analyze how this student, Courtney Ainsworth, developed details through those two tools. She begins her paragraph with number 5 from the list of authors' sentences above (see p. 63).

Vendetta
by Courtney Ainsworth
(a student paper)

The condemned man's hands were behind his back, <u>the wrists bound with a cord</u>. (1) The man's eyes, *a penetrating violet color*, glanced around the crowd, *a motley crew of all types and walks of life who took perverse pleasure in watching suffering*. (2) The second condemned man to the right of him, <u>his eyes scrunched up tightly</u>, muttered quiet prayers to whatever deity would listen. (3) To the left stood the third condemned man, *a criminal greatly experienced but hitherto greatly unpunished in crime*. (4) After a nervous pause, the magistrate began to read off an account of the crimes the three accused men were being executed for, <u>murder topping the list</u>. (5) The crowd listened silently, <u>an oppressive, heavy silence and palpable discomfort permeating the scene</u>. (6) The first man's eyes began to dart around more quickly, scanning the crowd to pinpoint someone expected to be there, before setting on a slight woman standing to the side of the crowd. (7) <u>Eyes locking with hers</u>, he began to relax, <u>a smirk stretching his lips</u>. (8) The magistrate finished with a nervous cough, and after rolling up his piece of parchment, ordered the executioner to begin. (9) As the hangman started to pull the hoods over the first of the three men's heads, explosively a slight woman near the gallows started shrieking, *a shrill, loud sound that echoed and made the crowd cringe and glance about, an unwanted, uncomfortable distraction,* as twelve men near the slight woman abruptly drew their pistols and pointed them at the magistrate and executioner. (10) One of the twelve climbed the gallows and approached the prisoners, <u>knife grasped firmly in his large hand as he moved forward</u>, and swiftly cut the bonds on the men's hands before handing each of the three a pistol. (11) <u>Sneer larger than ever</u>, the main convict jumped off the gallows to the magistrate, ordering him to start walking, <u>a terrified expression on the magistrate's face</u>. (12) In a commotion in front of the gallows, the rescuers gathered the magistrate and the executioner, <u>the crowd impotent in stunned silence</u>. (13) The magistrate glanced nervously about the menacing twelve rescuers, <u>his expression showing astonishment at the number of men the convict had managed to corral to come to his rescue</u>. (14) <u>His leer becoming a malicious smile</u>, the convict thrust the magistrate down into a sitting position on the ground and began to bark demands.

THE DESCRIBER

You've learned how to improve your writing by identification (*the appositive tool*) and elaboration (*the absolute tool*). Another way is to provide lots of description to help your readers clearly picture what you are writing about. A sentence-composing tool that provides descriptive details is a *participle*, the describing tool.

There are two kinds of participles: one—*a present participle*—ends in *-ing*, and the other—*a past participle*—usually ends in *-ed*.

Look at these sentences to see how participles improve sentences by adding more descriptive details.

WITHOUT DESCRIBERS

He continued to concentrate on the dusty road.

Jody's father was a little bothered by it.

Smaug the Dragon lay, with wings folded like an immeasurable bat.

Harry blinked and looked down at the floor.

WITH DESCRIBERS (*-ing*)

<u>Grasp**ing** more firmly his newspaper-wrapped notebook and his tin-can lunch of cornbread and oil sausages</u>, he continued to concentrate on the dusty road.

> Mildred D. Taylor, *Roll of Thunder, Hear My Cry*

Jody's father, <u>watch**ing** the pony stop and start and trot and gallop</u>, was a little bothered by it.

> John Steinbeck, *The Red Pony*

WITH DESCRIBERS (-*ed*)

> Smaug the Dragon lay with wings folded like an immeasurable bat,
> <u>turn**ed** partly to one side so that the hobbit could see his underparts.</u>
>
> J. R. R. Tolkien, The Hobbit

> <u>Blind**ed** by the blaze of the spells that had blasted from every direction,</u>
> Harry blinked and looked down at the floor.
>
> J. K. Rowling, Harry Potter and the Goblet of Fire

> **Remember this:** Participles are sentence parts that describe. Some of them, called *present participles*, end in *-ing*. Others, called past participles, usually end in *-ed*.

Every participle is removable. If an **-ing** or **-ed** phrase is **not** removable, it's not a participle. Which two sentences below contain participles because the underlined part can be removed without destroying the rest of the sentence?

1. The runner, <u>nearing the finish line</u>, stumbled.

2. The runner was <u>nearing the finish line</u>.

3. The dog, <u>covered with mud</u>, jumped on the sofa.

4. The dog was <u>covered with mud</u>.

ACTIVITY 1

Match the participle with the sentence. Write out each sentence, underlining the participle. Notice the three places participles occur in a sentence: *opener, S-V split, closer.*

Sentences	Participles
1. In the other narrow bed, his brother went on sleeping, ^ . Gina Berriault, "The Stone Boy"	**a.** pinned for a moment to the sky with his father's bullet
2. I took a turn at the oyster table, ^ . Pat Conroy, *South of Broad*	**b.** holding a hand before her eyes so that other patients and visitors should not see
3. ^ , he soon had a roaring fire over which he thawed the ice from his face. Jack London, "To Build a Fire"	**c.** undisturbed by the alarm clock's rusty ring
4. The bird, ^ , was suspended in midair, and then it fell. Kate DiCamillo, *The Tiger Rising*	**d.** working carefully from a small beginning
5. ^ , she began to weep. J. M. Coetzee, *Life and Times of Michael K*	**e.** prying the oyster loose from its shells with the blunt-nosed knife

ACTIVITY 2

Combine two sentences into just one sentence. Make the underlined part a participle to insert at the caret (^) in the first sentence. Notice how participles use commas for the places where they can occur in a sentence: *opener, S-V split, closer*.

EXAMPLE

Opener Participle:

^ , she found a bag full of Lego blocks of all shapes and sizes. She was <u>rummag**ing** on the top shelf of her closet</u>.

Combined: <u>Rummaging on the top shelf of her closet</u>, she found a bag full of Lego blocks of all shapes and sizes.

Jostein Gaarder, *Sophie's World*

S-V Split Participle:

The tent, ^ , glowed warmly in the midst of the plain. The tent was <u>illumin**ed** by candle light</u>.

Combined: The tent, <u>illumin**ed** by candle light</u>, glowed warmly in the midst of the plain.

Jack London, "To Build a Fire"

Closer Participle:

Suddenly the shark soared up out of the water in a fountain of spray, ^ . The shark was <u>turn**ing** as he fell</u>.

Combined: Suddenly the shark soared up out of the water in a fountain of spray, <u>turn**ing** as he fell</u>.

Willard Price, "The Killer Shark"

OPENER PARTICIPLES

1. ^ , I came across a bear cub separated from its mother. I was <u>walking along in a lonesome glen</u>.

    Keith Donohue, *The Stolen Child*

2. ^ , she was seen ceaselessly wandering around the little village. She was <u>bathed in tears</u>.

    Alexander Dumas, *The Count of Monte Cristo*

3. ^ , Mortenson stepped off ice and onto solid ground for the first time in more than three months. He was <u>picking his way down a narrow gorge</u>.

    Greg Mortenson, *Three Cups of Tea*

4. ^ , I switched to the more portable flute. I was <u>dismayed at how difficult it was to carry a heavy cello that half mile to school</u>.

    Perri Knize, *A Piano Odyssey*

5. ^ , she would lead me around the room in an impromptu waltz. She was <u>lifting me off the floor by my skinny shoulders</u>.

    Judith Ortiz Cofer, *Silent Dancing*

S-V SPLIT PARTICIPLES

6. The hangman, ^ , produced a small cotton bag like a flour bag and drew it down over the prisoner's face. The hangman was <u>standing on the gallows</u>.

    George Orwell, "A Hanging"

7. His tiny feet, ^ , would have neatly fitted into a delicate lady's dancing slippers. The feet were <u>encased in short black boots with steel buckles</u>.

    Truman Capote, *In Cold Blood*

8. The rain, ^ , bounced in the wet street. The rain was <u>falling straight down</u>.

   Wallace Stegner, *Crossing to Safety*

9. Romey's fried ham and Devola's biscuits, ^ , had sustained us. The ham and biscuits were <u>slathered thick with real butter and honey</u>.

   Bill and Vera Cleaver, *Where the Lilies Bloom*

10. Professor Kazan, ^ , was the first ashore. He was <u>wearing a spotlessly white tropical suit and a wide-brimmed hat</u>.

    Arthur C. Clarke, *Dolphin Island*

CLOSER PARTICIPLES

11. It went slowly down the road, ^ . It was <u>taking its time</u>.

    Brian W. Aldiss, "Who Can Replace a Man?"

12. Our reunion with Mother in California was a joyous festival, ^ . The reunion was <u>studded with tears, hugs, and lipsticked kisses</u>.

    Maya Angelou, *The Heart of a Woman*

13. Meanwhile, she sat stiffly in the chair, ^ . She was <u>trying not to show the pain it caused her</u>.

    Eleanor Coerr, *Sadako and the Thousand Paper Cranes*

14. Down the slope Becky halted and was staring upward at him, ^ . Becky was <u>worried</u>.

    John Updike, "Man and Daughter in the Cold"

15. She sat in a rocking chair, her long legs curled under her, ^ . She was <u>looking very calm and composed</u>.

    Michael Crichton, *Travels*

ACTIVITY 3

To practice creating participles, substitute a new participle for the existing underlined one.

EXAMPLES

Author's Present Participle: We turned our heads in the direction of the sound, but it was only a car, one of those small foreign cars, brilliant red, <u>making as much noise as a Mack truck</u>.

> Robert Cormier, *Take Me Where the Good Times Are*

Student's Present Participle: We turned our heads in the direction of the sound, but it was only a car, one of those small foreign cars, brilliant red, <u>squealing around the sharp curve dangerously at 60 miles per hour</u>.

Author's Past Participle: Slowly, <u>filled with dissatisfaction</u>, he had gone to his room and got into bed.

> Betsy Byars, *The Summer of the Swans*

Student's Past Participle: Slowly, <u>exhausted from the summer heat at the construction site</u>, he had gone to his room and got into bed.

1. <u>Backing from under the porch on his hands and knees</u>, he touched the lantern and tipped it over.

> William H. Armstrong, *Sounder*

2. For two nights and days, <u>imprisoned in his crate</u>, Buck neither ate nor drank.

> Jack London, *The Call of the Wild*

3. Major Arthur Godfrey Peuchen, <u>starting to undress for sleeping</u>, thought the sound of the *Titanic* hitting the iceberg was like a train crash.

   Walter Lord, *A Night to Remember*

4. He turned from the mountains and looked at the sheep, <u>scattered over the little meadow</u>.

   Hal Borland, *When the Legends Die*

5. We plodded along with the cold mud against our feet, <u>walking faster and faster to reach the crossroads</u>.

   Mildred D. Taylor, *Roll of Thunder, Hear My Cry*

ACTIVITY 4

Unscramble and write out the sentence parts to imitate the model sentence. Then write a sentence of your own that imitates all the sentence parts of the model, not just the participles.

EXAMPLE

Model Sentence: They stood motionless and silent, listening.

   Gaston Leroux, *The Phantom of the Opera*

Scrambled Sentence Parts:

a. remained

b. they

c. hoping

d. quiet but anxious

Unscrambled Imitation: They remained quiet but anxious, hoping.

Sample Student Imitation: She was beautiful and delightful, inspiring.

----

1. Discouraged, I hung up the phone and walked out into the woods behind the house.

    Jean Craighead George, *My Side of the Mountain*

    1a. I leaped across the room

    1b. and bolted out the door

    1c. into the emergency exit

    1d. terrified

2. A large woman, wearing faded overalls, got out and waddled over to them.

    Alexander Key, *The Forgotten Door*

    2a. and strolled over to him

    2b. the proud child

    2c. stood up

    2d. holding her drawing

3. They walked carefully across the vegetable garden, picking their way through rows of cabbages, beets, broccoli, pumpkins.

    Madeleine L'Engle, *A Wrinkle in Time*

    3a. working their way through scenes

    3b. of escape, violence, heartbreak, murder

    3c. they chatted intensely

    3d. about the TV series

4. Their heads were covered with wigs of European hair, curled in the latest fashion with ropes of pearls, rubies, and diamonds.

Margaret Landon, *Anna and the King of Siam*

    4a. with images of singers, drummers, and guitarists

    4b. colored with the wildest colors

    4c. their books were protected

    4d. with covers of dazzling material

5. When the knock came, Trudy walked onto the porch, where a stout woman waited, dressed in a flower skirt and a white blouse.

David Wroblewski, *Edgar Sawtelle*

    5a. bowed with a lovely curve and a plum color

    5b. after the rain stopped

    5c. where a drenched tree stood

    5d. Jen looked out the window

ACTIVITY 5

Imitate each model sentence—all of it, not just the underlined participle. Make your imitation so good that no one can tell which sentence is yours and which is the author's.

MODELS AND SAMPLE IMITATIONS

1. <u>Walking along in silence</u>, he had no regrets.

Paulo Coelho, *The Alchemist*

Sample: <u>Whistling alone in private</u>, Elsie had cheerful fantasies.

2. The exercise got the blood pumping through his brain, <u>numbed by the hours of lost sleep</u>.

    Frank Bonham, *Chief*

    Sample: The assignment started the student worrying about the essay, <u>translated by a Japanese student into English</u>.

3. I kept moving, <u>carrying the wounded people to the trees and up into the rocky ravine</u>.

    Daoud Hari, *The Translator*

    Sample: I stopped walking, <u>resting my tired feet on the chair and up over the table's edge</u>.

4. Cautiously, he removed a spider from its jar and let it walk back and forth across a dinner plate, <u>turning it with a pair of tweezers when it neared the edge</u>.

    Pat Conroy, *The Prince of Tides*

    Sample: Curiously, she observed the baby in its crib and noticed it turn left and right on its tiny mattress, <u>watching it with a look of love as it extended its hand</u>.

5. I reached the raft, let out all the rope and sat with my arms wrapped around my knees and my head down, <u>trying to put out the fire of fear that was blazing within me</u>.

    Yann Martel, *Life of Pi*

    Sample: I left the room, took all my supplies, and moved with a confidence driving my steps and a light heart, <u>wanting to start out on this journey of discovery that was waiting for me</u>.

ACTIVITY 6

Add a participle at each caret mark (^). The words that the participles describe are bolded. The last five sentences illustrate that good writers sometimes use more than one participle to describe the same thing in different ways.

EXAMPLE

> *Incomplete Sentence:* The **fire** burst the house and let it slam flat down, ^ .
>
> *Sample Participle:* The fire burst the house and let it slam flat down, <u>popping its roof off like the lid of a can.</u>
>
> *Original:* The fire burst the house and let it slam flat down, <u>puffing out skirts of spark and smoke.</u>
>
> Ray Bradbury, *The Martian Chronicles*

1. **Henry** reached and touched the monkey's fur, ^ .

   Yann Martel, *Beatrice and Virgil*

2. ^ , **he** jogged out of the yard.

   Marguerite Henry, *Misty of Chincoteague*

3. The **singer**, ^ , was as poorly dressed as the doctor's daughter was well dressed.

   Toni Morrison, *Song of Solomon*

4. At eleven o'clock **a man in a raincoat**, ^ , tapped at my front door and said that Mr. Gatsby had sent him over to cut my grass.

   F. Scott Fitzgerald, *The Great Gatsby*

5. ^ , **we** worked all morning in opposite parts of the woods.

    Truman Capote, *The Grass Harp*

6. **Flies** buzzed around their corpses, ^ , ^ .

    Stephen King, *The Stand*

7. **He** pulled down the coffins from their shelves, ^ , ^ .

    Neil Gaiman, *The Graveyard Book*

8. ^ and ^ , the mouse was running straight away from his field.

    Loren Eiseley, "The Brown Wasps"

9. **Mosquitoes** lit upon the exposed skin on my face, hands, and feet, ^ and ^ .

    Keith Donohue, *The Stolen Child*

10. **Children** love to play in piles of leaves, ^ , ^ .

    Diane Ackerman, *A Natural History of the Senses*

USING PARTICIPLES TO BUILD A PARAGRAPH

Write a paragraph that describes a tense situation, as in the paragraph (on pp. 79–80) by John Steinbeck.

WRITING PROCESS

Researching: The Steinbeck paragraph describes a family awake after a huge windy dust storm ended during the night. Study the model paragraph, identify all participles, and describe their length, position, and number (including several in the same sentence).

(1) Lying in their beds, the family heard the wind stop. (2) Slowly, they rose, wondering if the dust storm was over, murmuring their quiet

questions. (3) They went down the upstairs hall, padding softly in their bare feet on the cold floor, heading towards the kitchen, the meeting ground for family conferences. (4) When they were all assembled, no one spoke to break the silence, a blanket on the night. (5) Looking toward their father, the source of strength, they waited, listening, hoping, praying that the calm outside would last.

John Steinbeck, *The Grapes of Wrath*

Prewriting: Think of a real or imaginary event that lasted less than ten minutes, as in the model paragraph. Choose an event that communicates relief from a fearful or dangerous experience: a medical diagnosis, a near-miss auto accident, a tense incident with an angry person, or some other tense situation.

Drafting: Draft a paragraph describing what happened in that ten minutes. Within your paragraph, use participles in different places and lengths, and sometimes use more than one participle within the same sentence.

Peer responding and revising: Exchange your draft with other students in your class for suggestions to improve your paragraph, and give them suggestions, too. Then revise several times until your paragraph is finished.

Creating a title: Create a memorable title and subtitle, with a colon between them. Choose a title that your readers won't understand until after they read your paragraph. *Example:* "Aftermath: A Family Waits."

BUILDING PARAGRAPHS

You've learned and practiced a sentence-composing tool for identifying (*the appositive*); a tool for elaborating (*the absolute*); and a tool for describing (*the participle*). Now put all three tools to work to help build an opening paragraph for a story.

Pretend you are one of the authors below who has written the first sentence of a story that will take 300 pages to finish. Choose one of their sentences as the first sentence in a paragraph that will begin that 300-page story.

AUTHORS' SENTENCES

1. For a breathless time they sat there, silent and alert, with their backs turned to the wood-fire, each gazing into the shadows that encircled them.

    J. R. R. Tolkien, *The Fellowship of the Ring*

2. He sighed and donned a rubber apron, plugged himself into some final source of energy, and got busy with a gleaming array of vessels on a sink, linked by a system of glass and plastic tubing.

    Frank Bonham, *Chief*

3. Swelled to the top of its banks, clouded dark brown with silt, belching dirt and stones, and carrying blown branches along in its torrent, it had turned into an ugly, angered river.

    Bill and Vera Cleaver, *Where the Lilies Bloom*

4. The forest, darkened and dulled, stood motionless and silent on each side of the broad stream.

    Joseph Conrad, "The Lagoon"

5. Scrawny, blue-lipped, the skin around his eyes and the corners of his mouth a dark exploded purple, he looked like something an archeologist might find in the burial room of a pyramid, surrounded by his stuffed wives and pets, bedizened with his favorite jewels.

    Stephen King, *Bag of Bones*

6. He was twenty at the time, a tall young man in ill-fitting clothes, his hair very black and cut too short, his face a shade too thin, with dark whiskers, always showing no matter how often he shaved.

    Anne Tyler, *The Amateur Marriage*

7. At midmorning, the sailors had caught an enormous shark, which died on deck, thrashing wickedly in its death throes while no one dared go near enough to club it.

    Isabel Allende, *Daughter of Fortune*

8. Beside the entrance way, looking at her with dark, unblinking eyes, stood the biggest rat she had ever seen.

    Robert C. O'Brien, *Mrs. Frisby and the Rats of NIMH*

9. Papa sat on a bench in the barn, his broken leg stretched awkwardly before him, mending one of Jack's harnesses.

    Mildred D. Taylor, *Roll of Thunder, Hear My Cry*

10. It was a pitiful sight, the three of us in our overcoats and boots, standing among the dead stalks of winter.

    Cynthia Rylant, *Missing May*

Make up the rest of the paragraph, but somewhere in it use these sentence-composing tools:

- appositives, absolutes, and participles in various lengths (*short, medium, long*)

- appositives, absolutes, and participles in different places within the sentence (*opener, S-V split, closer*)

- multiple appositives or absolutes or participles within the same sentence

- mixture of different tools within the same sentence: appositives, absolutes, participles.

Important: You are just barely beginning a story, not writing a complete story. The complete story would require 300 pages from start to finish. Zoom in on just one detail in your first paragraph of that story—an object, a place, a mood, an event, a person—some detail triggered by what's in the author's sentence you chose from this list.

SAMPLE PAPER

Before drafting your own paragraph, study the appositives (*italicized*), absolutes (<u>underlined</u>), and participles (**bolded**) to analyze how the writer developed details through those three tools.

Heat

(1) Jan lay silent, **scarcely breathing**, <u>ears straining for the slightest sound</u>. (2) <u>A look of eerie concentration upon his face</u>, he scanned the surrounding area, **looking for any signs of movement**. (3) **Scanning**, he saw no movement, nothing except the trees and the wide open fields of an endless forest. (4) **Untouched**, the snow-covered ground glistened in the morning light, and the trees, *a line-up of black skeletons on the horizon*, swayed noisily in the wind. (5) Jan continued to scan the area, <u>his face turning red from the bitter cold</u>, <u>a nasal drip running out of his nose and freezing on his upper lip</u>. (6) ***Trying to make as little noise as possible***, *a secret hunter awaiting his prey*, he reached his hand into his back pocket and pulled out a handkerchief, *an already very messy piece of cloth*, and wiped his runny nose. (7) **Stretched back to place the soiled rag into his back pocket**, his hand moved quickly back and forth on his pants, **creating just enough heat to relieve his numb fingers from their pain for a few more minutes**. (8) The bitter cold was now invading his layered clothing, *special outfitters stuff for hunters bought from the Land's End catalog*, and most of his body was becoming numb, *mainly his hands, his feet, his arms, his legs, and his face*. (9) **Covered in four layers of clothing with no chance of beating the cold**, his body was stiffening from the bitter cold. (10) Jan struggled to deny what was happening, *the terror*

of freezing, but couldn't. (11) **Determined to persist in hope**, he remained vigilant, <u>eyes and ears alert for any movement or sound from beyond the thicket</u>. (12) **Buried halfway in snow**, Jan scanned the environment and fixated on a rustling sound in a nearby bush. (13) **Shaking back and forth**, whatever it was seemed possessed by some frantic need, *perhaps a desperate foraging for food*. (14) He watched closely, <u>eyes unwaveringly fixed on the target</u>, and reached slowly for the rifle beside him. (15) He held it firmly with both hands, <u>his left hand balancing it</u>, <u>his right hand placed on the trigger</u>. (16) As a deer emerged, *a small brown fawn with white spots and a furry white tail*, he centered his aim on the source of the rustling in the bush, <u>his knife ready to plunge into the fawn's body to open its warm guts</u>, *a furnace to warm his own freezing body*. (17) The deer appeared alert for predators, <u>its head rotating spasmodically back and forth</u>, **searching the ground for anything that could fill its empty stomach**, <u>the forest bereft of leaves</u>, <u>of pine needles</u>, <u>of anything that might resemble the usual stuff to sustain a deer's life</u>. (18) Jan, **trying not to startle the creature into bolting**, slowly crept closer for a better angle and a sure shot, *a precise bead from which to fell the animal*, and, then from the warmth of its innards, restore his own body's warmth. (19) **Slowly raising his rifle**, <u>the deer within his sight and close enough for the kill</u>, Jan pulled the trigger. The forest echoed the blast, then suddenly stilled. (20) The animal fell, **twitching on its side**, <u>its legs kicking in useless protest against the uncaring snow</u>, <u>blood oozing from the deer's head and reddening and staining the pure snow</u>. (21) Jan, **feeling a rush of sadness**, pulled out his knife from its sheath, <u>the sadness replaced by heat lust</u>.

THE COMBO

Sometimes things go better together. Fast food restaurants feature discounts for combos of sandwich, fries, and drink. Online stores advertise "better together" combo bargains for related items—books, clothes, shoes, and more. In composing sentences, a combo is using the identifier (*appositive*), the elaborator (*absolute*), or the describer (*participle*) within the same sentence, usually a mix of two, but sometimes all three.

Look at these sentences to see how combos improve sentences.

WITHOUT COMBOS

There were two people.

It was good to sit there in Charley's kitchen.

Several of them remember hiking with George.

He spent three days propped up in bed.

WITH COMBOS (*underlined*)

There were two people there, <u>a man and a woman</u>, <u>eating sandwiches while they stood up</u>. ***Combo: one identifier (appositive), one describer (participle)***

Michael Crichton, *Prey*

It was good to sit there in Charley's kitchen, <u>my coat and tie flung over a chair</u>, <u>surrounded by soul food and love</u>. ***Combo: one elaborator (absolute), one describer (participle)***

Eugenia Collier, "Sweet Potato Pie"

Several of them remember hiking with George, <u>his long hair braided</u>, <u>carrying an ice ax</u>, <u>wearing nothing but net long johns</u>. ***Combo: one elaborator (absolute), two describers (participles)***

Kenneth Brower, The Starship and the Canoe

He spent three days propped up in bed, <u>listening to the radio</u>, <u>reading comic books</u>, <u>and barking orders for Cokes</u>, <u>root beers</u>, <u>ginger ale</u>, <u>ice cream</u>, <u>and anything else he could think of</u>, while poor Mary Margaret, <u>a worrier from birth</u>, wandered from room to room. ***Combo: three describers (participles), one identifier (appositive)***

Fannie Flagg, Standing in the Rainbow

> **Remember this:** Combos are two or more *different* tools within the same sentence: the identifier (*appositive*), the elaborator (*absolute*), the describer (*participle*). Used occasionally within sentences, combos add variety, content, style, texture.

ACTIVITY 1

Match the combo with the sentence. Write out each sentence, underlining the combo. Notice all the places combos occur in a sentence. Combos with a slash mark (/) indicate different places in the sentence for the combo's tools.

Sentences	Combos
1. Ratz, ^ , filled a tray of glasses with draft Kirin beer. William Gibson, *Neuromancer*	**a.** his trousers rolled up, measuring the skeleton with a length of line

2. Many fishermen were around the skiff looking at what was lashed beside it, and one was in the water, ^ .

Ernest Hemingway,
The Old Man and the Sea

b. a fat woman with a white face / gazing into the street, her thick white arms folded under her loose breast

3. ^ , he looked like something an archeologist might find in the burial room of a pyramid, ^ .

Stephen King, *Bag of Bones*

c. tending bar, his prosthetic arm jerking monotonously

4. ^ , Phyllis was with her father when her mother called her to come and see Neil Armstrong, ^ , set foot on the moon.

Frank McCourt, *Teacher Man*

d. blue-lipped, the skin around his eyes and the corners of his mouth a dark exploded purple / surrounded by his stuffed wives and pets, bedizened with his favorite jewels

5. All the time he was reading the paper, his wife, ^ , leaned out of the window, ^ .

Bernard Malamud,
"A Summer's Reading"

e. concerned with her father who lay dying in the bedroom, but not wanting to miss the moon landing / the famous astronaut

ACTIVITY 2

Each author's sentence contains a combo. Identify the underlined tools. If you need to review the tool, study the pages below.

TOOLS	REVIEW THESE PAGES
The Identifier (*appositive*)	pages 35–49
The Elaborator (*absolute*)	pages 50–66
The Describer (*participle*)	pages 67–84

Sentences 1–5 contain two different tools. Sentences 6–10 contain all three different tools.

1. The bus doors opened with a wheeze, <u>letting off two dark-eyed young women</u>, <u>one of them obviously pregnant</u>.

   Anne Tyler, *Back When We Were Grownups*

2. She leaned down long enough to retrieve her diaphanous shawl and disappeared, <u>her arm raised so that the shawl trailed behind her</u>, <u>a shimmering banner</u>.

   Sara Gruen, *Water for Elephants*

3. Ruby drove the hogs and little sheep, <u>two of them dark</u>, <u>shooing them onto the slopes of Cold Mountain to fend for themselves through the autumn</u>.

   Charles Frazier, *Cold Mountain*

4. The interior of the log house, <u>designed in the grand *rancho* style of the 1980s</u>, featured a gargantuan living room, intricate log notches, <u>the distant mountains fitting artfully into the vast window</u>, against which birds broke their heads.

   Annie Proulx, "Man Crawling Out of Trees"

5. <u>A very slow speaker</u>, <u>averaging about a hundred words a minute</u>, Daniel Webster combined the musical charm of his deep organ-like voice, an ability to crush his opponents with a barrage of facts, a confident and deliberate manner of speaking, and a striking appearance to make his speeches a magnet that drew crowds.

   John F. Kennedy, *Profiles in Courage*

6. My father was an intimidating giant of a man, <u>a former college football player</u>, <u>standing six foot two and 245 pounds</u>, with thick, meaty hands, <u>every finger broken and bent</u>.

   Perri Knize, *A Piano Odyssey*

7. Ray-Ray leaped into the air, <u>his arms flung up</u>, but the ball was way over his head, <u>bouncing beyond him on the sidewalk near a woman</u>, <u>a mom who was jouncing a baby carriage at the door of the apartment house opposite</u>.

   Murray Heyert, "The New Kid"

8. Polly Chalmers, <u>the lady who ran the sewing shop</u>, was standing out on the sidewalk, <u>hands on her admirably slim hips</u>, <u>looking at the awning with an expression that seemed to be equally puzzled and admiring</u>.

   Stephen King, *Needful Things*

9. I didn't recognize her in the cover photograph, <u>a plump woman with big round glasses</u>, sitting beside him in the football stadium, <u>a single plaid blanket on their knees</u>, <u>both of them yelling and waving pennants</u>.

   Tobias Wolff, *Old School*

10. Georgie walked down the four steps to the cellar shelf, <u>the hair on the nape of his neck standing at attention</u>, <u>his hands cold</u>, sure that at any moment the cellar door would swing shut on its own, <u>closing off the white light falling through the kitchen windows</u>, and then he would hear IT, <u>the hidden monster</u>, <u>growling deeply in those lunatic seconds before it pounced on him and unzipped his guts</u>.

    Stephen King, *It*

ACTIVITY 3

Combine two sentences into just one sentence. Make the underlined parts a combo to insert at the carets (^) in the first sentence. Identify the combo's tools: *appositive*, *absolute*, or *participle*.

EXAMPLES

^ , my mother wandered by and stood in the doorway, ^ . My mother had <u>a dust rag in her hand</u>. She was <u>listening intently</u>.

Combined: <u>A dust rag in her hand</u>, my mother wandered by and stood in the doorway, <u>listening intently</u>.

Keith Donohue, *The Stolen Child*

Combo Tools: absolute (*a dust rag in her hand*), participle (*listening intently*)

1. He was sitting on his cot, ^ , ^ . He had <u>his elbows on his knees</u>. He was <u>looking down</u>.

   John Knowles, *A Separate Peace*

2. After the tyrannosaur's head crashed against the hood of the Land Cruiser and shattered the windshield, Tim was knocked flat on the seat, ^ , ^ . Tim was <u>blinking in the darkness</u>. His face showed <u>his mouth warm with blood</u>.

   Michael Crichton, *Jurassic Park*

3. The bartender had an artificial arm that was a Russian military prosthesis, ^ , ^ . The arm was <u>a seven-function force-feedback manipulator</u>. It was <u>cased in grubby pink plastic</u>.

   William Gibson, *Neuromancer*

4. Boo Boo Tannenbaum, ^ , came into the kitchen, ^ , ^ . Boo Boo was <u>the lady of the house</u>. She was <u>a small</u>, <u>almost hipless girl of twenty-five</u>. She was <u>dressed in knee-length jeans and a black turtleneck pullover</u>.

J. D. Salinger, "Down at the Dinghy"

5. ^ , the couple began to tell each other the stories of their lives, ^ , ^ . The couple was <u>staring at each other inside the rowboat</u>. The stories were <u>the ones that really mattered</u>. The stories included <u>the ones that remain secret until the right boy comes around the corner or the perfect girl comes walking down the street</u>.

Pat Conroy, *South of Broad*

ACTIVITY 4

To create combos, substitute a new tool for each existing underlined tool. Identify the tools in the combo.

EXAMPLES

Author's Combo: Rose Kennedy loved Paris, and she swirled into the city after I'd been there a few weeks, <u>taking a suite at a favorite hotel</u>, <u>the Ritz</u>. (*combo: present participle, appositive*)

Edward M. Kennedy, *True Compass*

Student's Combo: Rose Kennedy loved Paris, and she swirled into the city after I'd been there a few weeks, <u>revisiting the art at the famous Louvre</u>, <u>a favorite</u>. (*combo: present participle, appositive*)

1. <u>Strapped to a bed in a Memphis hotel,</u> <u>his talent burning out micron by micron,</u> he hallucinated for thirty hours.

   William Gibson, *Neuromancer*

2. Mortenson stood by the drinking fountain of the high school, <u>the reeking trash can covering his head,</u> <u>listening as laughter faded down the hallway.</u>

   Greg Mortenson, *Three Cups of Tea*

3. Pale and drawn, <u>his brown hair unkempt,</u> Bob spoke only in monosyllables, <u>avoiding eye contact.</u>

   Dina Ingber, "Computer Addicts"

4. A male tiger was crouching, <u>staring dead ahead,</u> <u>ears swiveled around,</u> <u>every hair bristling.</u>

   Yann Martel, *Beatrice and Virgil*

5. She had one good friend in town, <u>a Puerto Rican woman named Lupe,</u> <u>a sprightly and rambunctious woman in her early seventies,</u> <u>dressed always in too-tight clothes on her plump body.</u>

   Oscar Hijuelos, *The Fourteen Sisters of Emilio Montez O'Brien*

ACTIVITY 5

For each model sentence, write the letter of its imitation. Then write your own imitation of the same model.

GROUP 1: MODEL SENTENCES

1. The bus doors opened with a wheeze, letting off two dark-eyed young women, one of them obviously pregnant.

   Anne Tyler, *Back When We Were Grownups*

2. She leaned down long enough to retrieve her diaphanous shawl and disappeared, her arm raised so that the shawl trailed behind her, a shimmering banner.

    Sara Gruen, *Water for Elephants*

3. Ruby drove the hogs and little sheep, two of them dark, shooing them onto the slopes of Cold Mountain to fend for themselves through the autumn.

    Charles Frazier, *Cold Mountain*

4. The interior of the log house, designed in the grand *rancho* style of the 1980s, featured a gargantuan living room, intricate log notches, the distant mountains fitting artfully into the vast window, against which birds broke their heads.

    Annie Proulx, "Man Crawling Out of Trees"

5. A very slow speaker, averaging about a hundred words a minute, Daniel Webster combined an ability to crush his opponents with a barrage of facts, and a confident manner of speaking to make his speeches a magnet that drew crowds.

    John F. Kennedy, *Profiles in Courage*

GROUP 1: IMITATIONS

a. The teacher spoke out loud enough to quiet her unruly class and continued, her voice raised so that the class looked toward her, a quieted assembly.

b. A very charismatic star, completing only a few movies in his lifetime, James Dean blended a feral intensity to add magnetism to his adolescent good looks, and a brooding way of acting to make his portrayals a commentary that spoke volumes.

c. The sudden laughter erupted like a song, sending out lovely light musical signals, all of them delightfully joyful.

d. Jason handled the food and available beverages, most of them beer and wine, putting them in front of the guests at the reception to enjoy with food at the party.

e. The reason for the long lecture, delivered by the irritated grandparent of the culprit, was a broken valuable plate, a spilled drink, the guilty rascal fidgeting nervously during his reprimand, from which the boy learned his punishment.

GROUP 2: MODEL SENTENCES

6. Ray-Ray leaped into the air, his arms flung up, but the ball was way over his head, bouncing beyond him on the sidewalk near a woman, a mom who was jouncing a baby carriage at the door of the apartment house opposite.

   Murray Heyert, "The New Kid"

7. My father was an intimidating giant of a man, a former college football player, standing six foot two and 245 pounds, with thick, meaty hands, every finger broken and bent.

   Perri Knize, *A Piano Odyssey*

8. One structure, rejected at first as a monstrosity, became the World Fair's emblem, a machine huge and terrifying, eclipsing instantly the tower of Alexandre Eiffel that had so wounded America's pride.

   Eric Larson, *The Devil in the White City*

9. I didn't recognize her in the cover photograph, a plump woman with big round glasses, sitting beside him in the football stadium, a single plaid blanket on their knees, both of them yelling and waving pennants.

    Tobias Wolff, *Old School*

10. Georgie walked down the four steps to the cellar shelf, the hair on the nape of his neck standing at attention, his hands cold, sure that at any moment the cellar door would swing shut on its own, closing off the white light falling through the kitchen windows, and then he would hear IT, the hidden monster, growling deeply in those lunatic seconds before it pounced on him and unzipped his guts.

    Stephen King, *It*

GROUP 2: IMITATIONS

f. One performer, ignored at first as a joke, became the high school's favorite, a mascot funny and entertaining, outperforming easily the cheerleaders for all the teams who had so counted on winning.

g. I reminisced about him during the long summer, a cute lacrosse player with piercing blue eyes, laughing with me in the crowded cafeteria, a shared chocolate milk on our trays, both of us slurping and exchanging glances.

h. Samantha walked across the golden beach to the crystal ocean, the sand on the soles of her feet shifting under her steps, her heart light, hopeful that in one moment the beckoning ocean would enclose her in its reach, erasing all the painful memories churning inside her tired mind, and then she would feel relief, the cleansing refuge, arising gently in those magic moments as the water enveloped her and cleansed her psyche.

i. Carmela walked onto the stage, her voice warmed up, but the audience was distracted from her performance, staring around them at a heckler in the balcony, a guy who was drinking a small flask in the middle of her opening song onstage.

j. My favorite was a blossom of a girl, a lovely small Asian dancer, standing four feet and one hundred pounds, with tiny, graceful movements, each step serene and gentle.

ACTIVITY 6

Add a tool at each caret mark (^) to create a combo consisting of at least two different tools: *appositive*, *absolute*, *participle*.

EXAMPLE

Incomplete Sentence: ^ , ^ , she had been accepted by a good family of strict Spaniards whose name was old and respected, although their fortune had been lost long before my birth.

Sample Addition (*participle plus absolute*)*:* Encouraged by her welcome into his family, her engagement set soon afterward, she had been accepted by a good family of strict Spaniards whose name was old and respected, although their fortune had been lost long before my birth.

Original (*participle plus appositive*)*:* Married at an early age, an unspotted lamb, she had been accepted by a good family of strict Spaniards whose name was old and respected, although their fortune had been lost long before my birth.

Judith Ortiz Cofer, *Silent Dancing*

1. He handed me a bound black notebook, ^ , ^ .

> Keith Donohue, *The Stolen Child*

2. She remembered people crowded around a green table, ^ , ^ .

> Barbara Kingsolver, *Pigs in Heaven*

3. Hagrid, ^ , came striding toward them, ^ .

> J. K. Rowling, *Harry Potter and the Chamber of Secrets*

4. The book lover has a few books or many, ^ , ^ , ^ .

> Mortimer Adler, "How to Mark a Book"

5. The only happiness you have is writing something new, ^ , ^ , ^ .

> Lorrie Moore, *Self Help*

REVIEW

PART ONE

In each sentence below, find and identify one tool—appositive, absolute, present participle, or past participle.

1. Alfred pretended he hadn't heard the speaker, a big-shot politician he had never liked in high school.

> Robert Lipsyte, *The Contender*

2. Harry, fear spreading up his numb legs, watched Riddle stop between the high pillars and look up into the stone face of Slytherin, high above him in the half-darkness.

> J. K. Rowling, *Harry Potter and the Chamber of Secrets*

3. Huddled under my blankets, I observed the changing day, alone with my troubles.

    Keith Donahue, *The Stolen Child*

4. Dotted with sticker bushes, tumbleweed, and coiled rattlesnakes, the desert around our house seems to have no reason for existence, other than providing a place for people to dump things they no longer want, like tires and mattresses.

    Andre Agassi, *Open: An Autobiography*

5. There used to be this very kindly farmer who'd pass on the road, a Mennonite fellow I always remembered for his happiness.

    Oscar Hijuelos, *The Fourteen Sisters of Emilio Montez O'Brien*

6. The hanged prisoner was dangling with his toes pointed straight downward, revolving very slowly, as dead as a stone.

    George Orwell, "A Hanging"

7. In the root cellar, embedded in layers of clean sand, there were beets and carrots.

    Bill and Vera Cleaver, *Where the Lilies Bloom*

8. Winston Smith, his chin nuzzled into his breast in an effort to escape the vile wind, slipped quickly through the glass doors of Victory Mansion, though not quickly enough to prevent a swirl of gritty dust entering along with him.

    George Orwell, *1984*

9. Along the road, a stocky woman walked, carrying an apple box of dirty clothes toward the wash tubs.

    John Steinbeck, *The Grapes of Wrath*

10. On this fateful Wednesday, lulled by the sun, by the gentle sound of the tennis ball, by the steady drone of Pittinger's voice, by the fact that there were just two minutes to go, my mind slowly drifted off into a golden haze.

> Jean Shepherd, "A Fistful of Fig Newtons"

PART TWO

In each sentence below, find and identify <u>two or more tools</u>—appositive, absolute, present or past participle.

11. I started making an iceball, a perfect one from perfectly white snow, squeezed perfectly translucent so no snow remained all the way through.

> Annie Dillard, *An American Childhood*

12. When Columbus and his sailors came ashore, carrying swords, speaking oddly, the Arawak Indians ran to greet them, brought them food, water, gifts.

> Howard Zinn, *A People's History of the United States*

13. Polly Chalmers, the lady who ran the sewing shop, was standing out on the sidewalk, hands on her admirably slim hips, looking at the awning with an expression that seemed to be equally puzzled and admiring.

> Stephen King, *Needful Things*

14. I remember District 8, an ugly urban place stinking of industrial fumes, the people housed in run-down tenements, a blade of grass barely in sight.

> Suzanne Collins, *Catching Fire*

15. Paintings of Alek's ancestors, the family who had ruled Austria for six hundred years, lined the hallway, their subjects staring down with unreadable expressions.

   Scott Westerfield, *Leviathan*

16. The pony's tracks were plain enough, dragging through the frostlike dew on the young grass, the tired tracks with little lines between them where the hoofs had dragged.

   John Steinbeck, *The Red Pony*

17. There were three men, all in dark suits, standing on the front porch.

   Gary Paulsen, *The River*

18. About a hundred more goblins were sitting on high stools behind a long counter, scribbling in large ledgers, weighing coins in brass scales, examining precious stones through eyeglasses.

   J. K. Rowling, *Harry Potter and the Sorcerer's Stone*

19. Her mother was the short-order cook at the Comanche Cafe, the dirtiest, darkest, smelliest place in town, patronized by coal miners who never washed their faces and sometimes had such dangerous fights after drinking dago red that the sheriff had to come.

   Jean Stafford, "Bad Characters"

20. I'm sure he would keep me alive as long as he possibly could, my body deteriorating, disintegrating around me, dissolving until there's nothing left but my brain floating in a glass jar filled with clear liquid, my eyeballs drifting at the surface and tubes feeding what remains.

   Garth Stein, *The Art of Racing in the Rain*

PART THREE

Compose an interesting sentence that contains what is described. Code the tools: *italicize appositives*, underline absolutes, **bold present participles**, and **bold plus underline past participles**.

21. A long appositive for the beginning of your sentence

22. A long absolute for the end of your sentence

23. One present participle and one past participle, any position, any length anywhere in your sentence

24. Three *different* tools (*a combo*), any position, any length, anywhere in your sentence

25. Three *same* tools (*a multiple*), any position, any length, anywhere in your sentence

PART FOUR

Below is a basic paragraph about a conversation between a girl and a boy. Improve the paragraph by adding each of the four tools at least TWICE. *Italicize appositives*, underline absolutes, **bold present participles**, and **bold plus underline past participles**. In your revision you may add, change, or delete words.

PARAGRAPH TO REVISE

(1) Kander and Jasmine left the cafeteria together. (2) She was a perky junior with velvet brown eyes. (3) She was a new student who had transferred into his high school. (4) She had come from a school out-of-state. (5) Kander and Jasmine were strolling toward their math class third period. (6) The late bell was seconds away. (7) Kander was unfazed because he was hoping to extend their time together before the math test. (8) He said to her, "This geometry test is probably going to kill

me." (9) He said this in a low, mock-serious voice. (10) As he spoke, his mouth was turning into a slight grin. (11) Kander's eyes met hers. (12) He was trying to read her response. (13) He was wondering if she knew that the test stuff was just an excuse. (14) He wanted to keep on talking to her because she was the latest among the female population to make his heart leap. (15) Jasmine was smiling slightly. (16) Her right eyebrow was arching in a wordless response. (17) She was convinced that he was testing her. (18) She was glad.

USING COMBOS TO BUILD PARAGRAPHS

WRITING PROCESS

Researching: Think of a sports or entertainment event that ended triumphantly. You may choose to write about yourself, or about a famous athlete or entertainer. Choose an event where you can build your reader's interest in the outcome as you unfold the event for your readers: a victory in a close call game, a widely successful rock concert's conclusion, or some other event with a triumphant end.

Drafting: Draft one paragraph telling what happened in the triumphant event. Use a variety of sentence-composing tools: identifiers, elaborators, describers, combos.

Peer responding and revising: Exchange your draft with other students in your class for suggestions to improve your paragraph, and give them suggestions, too. Then revise several times until your paragraph is finished.

Creating a title: Create a memorable title that your readers won't understand until after they read your paragraph. *Example:* "Taffy Ball," a title for a paragraph about a basketball game with agile players whose bodies were like "taffy" because they moved in all directions.

Before drafting your own paragraph, study this sample paper. Notice Peter's use of the sentence-composing tools singly and in combos: appositives are *italicized*, absolutes <u>underlined</u>, present participles **bolded**, past participles **<u>bolded plus underlined</u>**.

Gold
by Peter Maleki
(*a student paper*)

<u>**Once unrecognized by many people**</u>, he used to be a nobody, *a young man so unknown that he might as well have never existed*. It wasn't until the 2008 Olympics that he became one of the most widely recognized athletes in the world. He won eight consecutive gold medals in one Olympic season, *an achievement unprecedented in the history of the Olympics*. His name was Michael Phelps. Phelps, *a native of Baltimore, Maryland*, had begun his career very early in his life. A *ten-year-old boy*, **<u>diagnosed with attention-deficit hyperactivity disorder</u>**, <u>his mind unable to stay focused in school</u>, Michael, *a kid swimmer*, discovered that he had natural talent as a swimmer, **holding the national records for his age group**. He qualified for the Olympics at age fifteen, *the youngest age for a male to qualify as an Olympic swimmer in over sixty-eight years*. When he was age fifteen and nine months, he broke the world record for the 200-meter butterfly, **becoming the youngest man ever to set a swimming record**. After having won many gold medals in various events, **including six gold medals in the 2004 Olympics**, he entered Beijing, ready to compete in the 2008 Olympics. **<u>Determined to do well</u>**, he nevertheless had no idea that he would go on to win eight gold medals, *the most medals that can be won by an athlete in a single season of the Olympics*. He competed unflinchingly, **winning one gold medal after another**, until he won them all. *Olympian gold-medalist unexcelled*, Michael Phelps became a worldwide Olympic superstar. There may never again be another Olympic champion receiving more global acclaim.

MORE TOOLS

In the previous sections, you learned, practiced, and applied appositives, absolutes, and participles—important sentence-composing tools that enhance the sentences of paragraphs. In this section, you'll do activities that include those and other tools to build sentences for strong paragraphs.

Based upon the popular novel *Twilight* by Stephenie Meyer, both paragraphs below describe the same trio of vampires, two men and one woman. Notice, though, how much more descriptive power is in the one with sentence-composing tools.

VERSION WITHOUT TOOLS

The man in front was easily the most beautiful. He was of a medium build. He smiled an easy smile. The woman was wilder. The second male hovered unobtrusively behind them. His eyes somehow seemed the most vigilant.

VERSION WITH TOOLS (*Underlined*)

The man in front was easily the most beautiful, his skin olive-toned beneath the typical pallor, his hair a glossy black. He was of a medium build, hard-muscled, but nothing next to Emmett's brawn from the other group of vampires. He smiled an easy smile, exposing a flash of gleaming white teeth. The woman was wilder, her eyes shifting restlessly between the men facing her and the loose grouping of the other group of vampires, her chaotic hair quivering in the slight breeze. The second male hovered unobtrusively behind them, slighter than the leader, his light brown hair and regular features both nondescript. His eyes, though completely still, somehow seemed the most vigilant, eyes not gold or black, but a deep burgundy color that was disturbing and sinister.

Obviously, the expanded paragraph is much stronger than the basic paragraph. In the following activities, you'll see that the authors usually expand their sentences to enrich the meaning and style of their paragraphs. Apply what you learn from this as you write your own expanded paragraphs.

ACTIVITY 1

Expand each sentence by adding sentence parts at the caret (^). The first five (1–5) have additions in one place; the next five (6–10) have additions in more than one place. Write out and punctuate the expanded sentence, underlining the added sentence parts.

Sentences	Sentence Parts
1. Then the efficient chaos, ^ , erupted. Stieg Larsson, *The Girl Who Kicked the Hornet's Nest*	**a.** drifting along the sides of houses, filling the roads
2. Outside, the snow kept falling, ^ . Kim Edwards, *The Memory Keeper's Daughter*	**b.** a black-and-white terrier mix
3. She had tied rags around her shoulders to keep out the spring chill and was picking through the trash while her dog, ^ , played at her feet. Jeannette Walls, *The Glass Castle*	**c.** a dilapidated "mansion" on Holmes Street in the heart of Kansas City
4. Mark Beckloff and I had just gone in on a house together, ^ . Dan Dye and Mark Beckloff, *Amazing Gracie: A Dog's Tale*	**d.** the same in every emergency room the world over

Sentences	Sentence Parts

5. ^ , the beautiful Scarlett O'Hara made a pretty picture.
 	
    Margaret Mitchell,
    Gone with the Wind
	e. seated with Stuart and Bret Tarleton on the cool shade of the porch of Tara, her father's plantation, that bright April afternoon of 1861

Sentences	Sentence Parts
6. The race track is dry for the pace lap, and then just after the green flag is waved, ^ , there is a wall of rain, ^ , and all of the cars spin out of control into the fields, and he drives through them as if the rain didn't fall on him, ^ . Garth Stein, *The Art of Racing in the Rain*	**a.** like most boys his age / especially around other boys / who all tried to act cool as if girls were some strange new species
7. ^ , he saw the eyes of the fifty children who had followed him, ^ , ^ . Greg Mortenson, *Three Cups of Tea*	**b.** when Mortenson looked up / ringing the opening in the ceiling as they lay on the roof / staring at the first foreigner they had ever seen in Korphe
8. ^ , Henry liked girls a lot more than he could bring himself to admit, ^ , ^ . Jamie Ford, *The Hotel at the Corner of Bitter and Sweet*	**c.** flooding the tile grooves / pooling around the rims of the squat toilets / dripping over the doorstep and into the dried-up garden behind the shack
9. ^ , ^ , I crept over to the bedroll and tried to find a comfortable place for my head, ^ . Sara Gruen, *Water for Elephants*	**d.** when Walter finished cleaning my cuts / removing glass from my hair / which was battered both front and back
10. Water was everywhere, ^ , ^ , ^ . Téa Obreht, *The Tiger's Wife*	**e.** indicating the start of the race / a torrential downpour that engulfs the track / like he had a magic spell that cleared the water from his path

ACTIVITY 2

In this series of activities, you'll practice adding sentence parts to sentences from the famous Harry Potter novels. For all your additions, pretend you are J. K. Rowling, the author, composing a sentence that will actually appear in a Harry Potter book destined to become a huge best-seller because of terrific sentences you helped write!

PART ONE

Each sentence below is a stripped-down version of a Harry Potter sentence. Expand the sentence at every caret mark (^). In parentheses is the number of words missing. Add about that number of words.

EXAMPLE

Basic Sentence: ^ , Harry spotted Fred and George Weasley, ^ .
(*7 words, 7 words*)

Sample Student Result: <u>Overhearing their muffled conversation near the dark lake around midnight</u>, Harry spotted Fred and George Weasley, <u>whose faces were pale and eerie in the moonlight</u>.

Original: <u>Through the thicket of legs around him</u>, Harry spotted Fred and George Weasley, <u>wrestling the rogue Bludger into a box</u>.

Harry Potter and the Chamber of Secrets

---

1. ^ and ^ , the giants brought themselves to the point of extinction by warring amongst themselves during the last century.
(*1 word, 1 word*)

Harry Potter and the Goblet of Fire

2. Harry leaned forward to see Hagrid, ^ , ^ .
   (*13 words, 11 words*)

   > *Harry Potter and the Prisoner of Azkaban*

3. Harry twisted his body around and saw a grindylow, ^ , ^ , ^ , ^ .
   (*5 words, 5 words, 8 words, 4 words*)

   > *Harry Potter and the Goblet of Fire*

4. ^ , something hit his side of the car with the force of a charging bull, ^ , ^ .
   (*4 words, 6 words, 9 words*)

   > *Harry Potter and the Chamber of Secrets*

5. ^ , ^ , ^ , Harry fell into an uneasy sleep.
   (*1 word, 2 words, 7 words*)

   > *Harry Potter and the Chamber of Secrets*

PART TWO

Expand each sentence at the caret mark (^) *three different ways* as in these examples.

EXAMPLES

> *Basic Sentence:* Twenty-four letters to Harry found their way into the house.

> *Adding sentence parts at the beginning of the sentence:*

1. <u>A record number for one day's delivery</u>, twenty-four letters to Harry found their way into the house.

2. <u>In the midst of a strange hurricane lasting only one minute</u>, twenty-four letters to Harry found their way into the house.

3. <u>Arriving against the wishes of Vernon and Petunia Dursley,</u> twenty-four letters to Harry found their way into the house.

Adding sentence parts at the middle of the sentence:

4. Twenty-four letters to Harry, <u>all delivered by the owl,</u> found their way into the house.

5. Twenty-four letters to Harry, <u>because he snuck them in from the mailbox,</u> found their way into the house.

6. Twenty-four letters to Harry, <u>addressed in code intelligible only to Harry,</u> found their way into the house.

Adding sentence parts at the end of the sentence:

7. Twenty-four letters to Harry found their way into the house, <u>despite the fact that Uncle Vernon had met the mailman every day and told Dudley to keep an eye on the back door.</u>

8. Twenty-four letters to Harry found their way into the house, <u>covered with dirt from Uncle Vernon's attempt to bury them in the back yard.</u>

9. Twenty-four letters to Harry found their way into the house, <u>a weird house with twenty-four rooms,</u> <u>twenty-four windows, and twenty-four doors but only one floor.</u>

Adding sentence parts at all three places:

10. <u>At the final count,</u> twenty-four letters to Harry, <u>none with return addresses,</u> found their way into the house, <u>delivered secretly by Dudley in exchange for Harry's offer to transform Dudley into a handsome prince.</u>

11.   <u>Amazingly</u>, twenty-four letters to Harry, <u>through the invisible courier hired from the wizard directory</u>, found their way into the house, <u>to the astonishment and furor of Uncle Vernon</u>.

12.   <u>Materializing out of nothing through Harry's special use-once-only spell for undetectable mail delivery</u>, twenty-four letters to Harry, <u>all written in invisible typing readable only with Harry's spectacles</u>, found their way into the house, <u>the final letter warning Harry of the presence of Lord Valdemort in Harry's neighborhood</u>.

Original Sentence: Twenty-four letters to Harry found their way into the house, rolled up and hidden inside each of the two dozen eggs that their very confused milkman had handed Aunt Petunia through the living room window.

Harry Potter and the Sorcerer's Stone

- -

1.   Like examples 1–3 above, expand this same sentence three different ways at the beginning of the sentence.

   ^ , a hooded figure came crawling across the ground like some stalking beast.

   Harry Potter and the Sorcerer's Stone

2.   Like examples 4–6 above, expand this same sentence three different ways at the middle of the sentence.

   Ron Weasley, ^ , came from a whole family of wizards.

   Harry Potter and the Prisoner of Azkaban

3.   Like examples 7–9 above, expand this same sentence three different ways at the end of the sentence.

   Harry was on his feet again, ^ .

   Harry Potter and the Order of the Phoenix

4. Like examples 10–12 above, expand this same sentence three different ways at the beginning, the middle, and the end of the sentence.

^ , a giant spider, ^ , was advancing on Ron, ^ .

Harry Potter and the Prisoner of Azkaban

BUILDING PARAGRAPHS

Expand the basic paragraph below by adding sentence parts in various places indicated by a caret mark (^), and adding some additional sentences at the end of the paragraph. Your goal is to create through your additions a memorable paragraph, one as good as those by author J. K. Rowling in the Harry Potter novels.

BASIC PARAGRAPH TO EXPAND

(1) Down the stairs came a heffle, ^ . (2) Harry had only seen a heffle once before, when he and Ron were in the remotest recesses of the Hogwarts dungeon, ^ . (3) He remembered the horrifying sound a heffle makes, ^ . (4) In Charms class, Professor Flitwick had taught them one spell that could disable a heffle, ^ , and now Harry was trying desperately to remember it. (5) At moments like this, Harry missed Hermione, ^ . (6) Now the heffle was halfway down the stairs, glaring directly at Harry, ^ . (7) ^ , the heffle started making the awful sound, and Harry, ^ , knew his time was running out. (8) ^ , a magic sword, ^ , was locked in the glass bookcase a few feet away from Harry, ^ . (FINISH YOUR PARAGRAPH BY ADDING ANYWHERE A FEW MORE SPECTACULAR SENTENCES.)

GOOD MARKS

Have you ever heard the expression "on the mark"? It means getting something exactly right. In writing, hitting something on the mark, including the just-right punctuation mark, can be as satisfying as shooting an arrow that hits the bull's-eye.

Using bull's-eye punctuation marks is the aim of this section. You already know how to use periods, commas, and question marks, but what about dashes and semicolons and colons? They are very good marks. Effective writers use those marks frequently in the sentences of their paragraphs because those good marks tell readers things that periods and commas don't. In the following activities, you'll learn and practice how authors use dashes and semicolons and colons, and use them in your own writing so that all your punctuation will be "on the mark" so that your sentences, and the paragraphs that contain them, will resemble the writing of authors.

From the reader's point of view, punctuation provides a map for one who must otherwise drive blindly past the by-ways, intersections, and detours of a writer's thought.

—Mina Shaughnessy

DASH TO INTERRUPT A SENTENCE

Sometimes a writer has an unplanned, sudden thought, so the writer interrupts a sentence to tell readers what it is.

One special punctuation mark interrupts a sentence—a dash. It indicates a spur-of-the-moment thought or an afterthought within a sentence.

A dash says to your readers, "Hey! Here's something I just thought of that you should know."

Here are a few examples. Notice that the writer uses dashes to alert readers to an abrupt shift in thought within the sentence.

EXAMPLES

1. Another subject—one you'll like—will occur to you. (*The interruption is a sudden thought in the middle of the sentence.*)

   Mary Ann Shaffer and Annie Barrows,
   The Guernsey Literary and Potato Peel Pie Society

2. When you looked across the land, everything you could see—the horizon, the river, the fence lines, the gullies, the scrub cedar—was spread out and flat. (*The interruption clarifies what could be seen across the land.*)

   Jeannette Walls, *Half Broke Horses*

3. Whenever Hester tried to use an upstairs bathroom—she felt that she was "family," and therefore not bound by the rules governing the guests—her mother told her that she would wait in line downstairs like everyone else. (*The interruption is an abrupt second sentence within the sentence.*)

   John Irving, *A Prayer for Owen Meany*

Dashes indicate abruptness—a shift in thought, a change of topics, a "P.S." or "BTW" within the same sentence. The interruption itself can be either a sentence or a sentence part. In sentences 1 and 3, it is a sentence; in sentence 2, a sentence part.

ACTIVITY 1

Match the interruption with the sentence it interrupts. Write the result.

Sentence	Interruption
1. She appeared to glow before him, and she was lovely—^. Ian McEwan, *On Chesil Beach*	**a.** a mixture of Georgia redbone hound and bulldog
2. The dog was not much to look at—^. William H. Armstrong, *Sounder*	**b.** beautiful, sensuous, gifted, good-natured beyond belief
3. Sarah gave Caleb a shell—^—that was curled and smelled of salt. Patricia MacLachlan, *Sarah, Plain and Tall*	**c.** a moon shell, she called it
4. Everything that I saw—^—filled me with happiness. Scott O'Dell, *Island of the Blue Dolphins*	**d.** simply the fact that he was breathing, that all his organs were in their proper places, that blood flowed quietly and effectively through his small, sturdy limbs
5. Her baby still had the power to stagger her at times—^. Jhumpa Lahiri, *Unaccustomed Earth*	**e.** the otter playing in the kelp, the rings of foam around the rocks that guarded the harbor, the gulls flying, the tides moving past the sandspit

ACTIVITY 2

Create an interruption for the sentence. Use dashes to indicate where the interruption occurs.

EXAMPLE

Incomplete: It had taken Crocker and his team—^—almost half a year to cross the plains and mountains.

Student Sample: It had taken Crocker and his team—**men and women from all walks of life and ages and abilities to endure that long trip**—almost half a year to cross the plains and mountains.

Original: It had taken Crocker and his team—**young men, all in good condition, with some money and supplies plus horses and wagons**—almost half a year to cross the plains and mountains.

Stephen E. Ambrose, *Nothing Like It in the World*

---

1. He beat the creature off with his hands—^—until he remembered his sword and drew it out.

   J. R. R. Tolkien, *The Hobbit*

2. Jim and I decided to auction off everything—^.

   Jeannette Walls, *Half Broke Horses*

3. When I passed the Radley Place for the fourth time that day—^—my gloom had deepened to match the house.

   Harper Lee, *To Kill a Mockingbird*

4. As for the terrors ahead—^—you just have to stand up to your fear and not let it squeeze you white.

   Katherine Paterson, *Bridge to Terabithia*

5. When I tackled him—^—it felt like I had slammed into the side of a mountain.

    Pat Conroy, *South of Broad*

6. The third day—^—Charles bounced a see-saw onto the head of a little girl and made her bleed, and the teacher made him stay inside all during recess.

    Shirley Jackson, "Charles"

7. The doctors of Monterey—^—were running crazy.

    John Steinbeck, *Cannery Row*

8. The apartment was on the top floor—^.

    F. Scott Fitzgerald, *The Great Gatsby*

9. A tremendous number of schoolgirls—^—crept into the hospital.

    John Hersey, *Hiroshima*

10. It is a difficult lesson to learn today—^.

    Anne Morrow Lindbergh, *Gift from the Sea*

SEMICOLON TO LINK TWO SENTENCES

Sometimes two sentences go better together because they both have something to say about the same person, place, object, idea, situation, and so forth.

One punctuation mark provides a way to link two consecutive sentences about a common topic; it's a semicolon.

A semicolon says to your readers, "These two sentences are linked in some way." Here are a few examples. Notice that the writer wants you to be alert for a link in meaning between the sentence pairs.

EXAMPLES

1. He did not understand change; he did not understand growth.
   (*The semicolon links two things he didn't understand.*)

   Thomas Wolfe, *Look Homeward, Angel*

2. His hand was swollen and heavy; a little thread of pain ran up
   the inside of his arm and settled in a pocket in his armpit. (*The
   semicolon links details of the injury to his hand.*)

   John Steinbeck, "Flight"

3. Percival, the smallest boy on the island, was mouse-colored
   and had not been very attractive even to his mother; Johnny,
   his brother, was well built, with fair hair and a natural
   belligerence. (*The semicolon links the contrast in the attractiveness
   of the brothers.*)

   William Golding, *Lord of the Flies*

ACTIVITY 3

Match the sentence linked by a semicolon to the first sentence. Write the
result.

First Sentence	Linked Sentence
1. With the force of a bullet, the wad of chewing gum shot out of the keyhole and straight down Peeve's left nostril; ^ . J. K. Rowling, *Harry Potter and the Prisoner of Azkaban*	**a.** the best zoos ran clinics little different from hospitals
2. Fenella hardly ever saw her grandma with her head uncovered; ^ . Katherine Mansfield, "The Voyage"	**b.** he whirled upright and zoomed away, cursing

3. She did not try to make her meals nauseating; ^ . Toni Morrison, *Song of Solomon*	**c.** she looked strange
4. The room was really dominated by a portrait, with its own light and a gilded frame; ^ . Alice Munro, "The Office"	**d.** it was of a good-looking, fair-haired man in middle age, sitting behind a desk, wearing a business suit, and looking preeminently prosperous, rosy, and agreeable
5. In the late twentieth century, veterinary medicine was scientifically advanced; ^ . Michael Crichton, *Jurassic Park*	**e.** she simply didn't know how not to

ACTIVITY 4

Create a second sentence to link to the given sentence. Use a semicolon to join the two sentences.

Directions for 1–5: Write a second sentence that tells what happened next. *Start the second sentence with the words provided.*

EXAMPLE

> *Incomplete:* I forced the last stone into its position; **I pounded ^ .**
>
> *Student Sample:* I forced the last stone into its position; **I pounded it into place with a sledgehammer.**

Original: I forced the last stone into its position; **I plastered it up.**

Edgar Allan Poe, "The Cask of Amontillado"

---

1. Instead of facing problems, one runs away; **one escapes ^ .**
   Anne Morrow Lindbergh, *Gift from the Sea*

2. The tyrannosaur bellowed angrily, and then the big hind leg came up and crashed down on the roof of the car; **the claws ^ .**
   Michael Crichton, *Jurassic Park*

3. He sat for a while with a stony face looking out the window; **then, he ^ .**
   Mildred D. Taylor, *Roll of Thunder, Hear My Cry*

4. A few stray white bread crumbs lay on the cleanly washed floor by the table; **putting a lamp upon a low stool, he ^ .**
   Sherwood Anderson, *Winesburg, Ohio*

5. The sound was like the scream of a rabbit caught in an owl's talons; **my flesh ^ .**
   Stephen King, *Bag of Bones*

Directions for 6–10: Write a second sentence that illustrates the first sentence. *Start the second sentence with the words provided.*

EXAMPLE

Incomplete: They were good children, bright children; **they ^ .**

Student Sample: They were good children, bright children; **they helped with the dishes, made their beds, and ran errands.**

Original: They were good children, bright children; **they did well in school and never got in serious trouble.**

Anne Tyler, *Saint Maybe*

----

6. She felt as if her body had shrunk; **it had ^ .**

Virginia Woolf, "Lappin and Lapinova"

7. Evening was advancing toward the island; **the sounds ^ .**

William Golding, *Lord of the Flies*

8. She had never seen anybody so charming and delightful; **the woman's heart ^ .**

Sarah Orne Jewett, "A White Heron"

9. She said she had some luggage and her children were sick; **they ^ .**

John Hersey, *Hiroshima*

10. She had a rare culinary gift; **she could ^ .**

Isabel Allende, *Daughter of Fortune*

Directions for 11–15: Write a second sentence that contrasts with the first sentence. *Start the second sentence with the words provided.*

EXAMPLE

Incomplete: There would be a pageant for the grown-ups; **there would be ^ .**

Student Sample: There would be a pageant for the grown-ups; **there would be for the kids opportunities to go outside to the playground and play on the jungle gym, swing, and sliding board.**

Original: There would be a pageant for the grown-ups; **there would be apple-bobbing, taffy-pulling, pinning the tail on the donkey for the children**.

Harper Lee, *To Kill a Mockingbird*

----

11. Her father's penmanship was small, precise, slightly feminine; **her mother's ^** .

Jhumpa Lahiri, *Unaccustomed Earth*

12. Grandfather lay drawn up in a ball, groaning so dreadfully that I felt a chill like cold water at the roots of my hair; **a moment or two after I came in, ^** .

Dorothy Canfield, "The Heyday of the Blood"

13. A man who was wise found that his wisdom was needed in every camp; **a man who was ^** .

John Steinbeck, *The Grapes of Wrath*

14. He had been standing, holding the reprint in his hand; **now he ^** .

Oliver La Farge, "The Little Stone Man"

15. If you look cute, you are cute; **if you look smart, ^** .

Betsy Byars, *The Summer of the Swans*

Directions for 16–20: Write a second sentence that is built like the first sentence, and join them together with a semicolon. *Start the second sentence with the words provided.*

EXAMPLE

Incomplete: When I worked nights, I wrote during the day; **when I ^ .**

Student Sample: When I worked nights, I wrote during the day; **when I went to sleep, I slept like a dead person.**

Original: When I worked nights, I wrote during the day; **when I worked days, I wrote during the night.**

Richard Wright, *American Hunger*

---

16. What she saw was certainly not for many eyes; **what she saw ^ .**
     James Baldwin, *Tell Me How Long the Train's Been Gone*

17. His neck was fat; **his throat ^ .**
     Hal Borland, *When the Legends Die*

18. Reporters started writing; **TV cameras ^ .**
     Barry Spacks, "Whoosh"

19. I remember that goat; **I ^ .**
     Wallace Stegner, *Wolf Willow*

20. If there was no beast—and almost certainly there was no beast—in that case, well and good; **if there was ^ .**
     William Golding, *Lord of the Flies*

COLON TO INTRODUCE A LIST

Good writers sometimes include a list within a sentence—of hobbies, of groceries, of cities, of parts of a computer, of colors, and so forth.

One punctuation mark provides a way to list a series of two or more items within a sentence; it's a colon.

A colon says to your readers, "Next in this sentence is the list of something just mentioned in the sentence." A writer uses a colon to alert readers to that upcoming list.

EXAMPLES

1. He didn't put any amount on it, just listed the things we took from the basement: a ham, four frozen chickens, four pounds of frozen butter, two quarts of honey, a peck of red yams. (*The colon signals that the things from the basement will be listed.*)

   Bill and Vera Cleaver, *Where the Lilies Bloom*

2. By the dawn, the house smelled of Sunday: chicken frying, bacon sizzling, and smoke sausages baking. (*The colon signals that the smells will be listed.*)

   Mildred D. Taylor, *Roll of Thunder, Hear My Cry*

3. Familiar objects settled into place around me: the drapes, pulled all the way back to let in air; the highly waxed coffee table with Mother's doodads bowing and shaking to the volume of Calvin's roaring voice; and Calvin, standing in center floor, smiling, awaiting his applause. (*The colon signals that the familiar objects will be listed.*)

   Rosa Guy, *The Friends*

Note: Whenever any item in a list is more than ten words or already contains a comma, use semicolons, not commas, to separate the items in the list. (*Number 3 above is an example.*)

Study these ten sentences to see what's on the left of a colon, and what's on the right of the colon. To the left of the colon must be a complete sentence that previews the list; to the right of the colon is that list. The bold part tells what the list will be.

1. **Their names** he knew: Thomas, Mary, Sally, Brooks.

     Alexander Key, *The Forgotten Door*

2. There were the **familiar trees** she knew so well at home: birches, pines, maples.

     Madeleine L'Engle, *A Wrinkle in Time*

3. In Maycomb, grown men stood outside in the front yard for only **two reasons**: death and politics.

     Harper Lee, *To Kill a Mockingbird*

4. I was assigned classes in English or **wherever a teacher was needed**: biology, art, physics, history, mathematics.

     Frank McCourt, *Teacher Man*

5. In my stillness, I began to notice **the animals**: strange birds with brilliant plumage, tree lizards with flickering blue tongues, and something that looked like a cross between a rat and a possum.

     Suzanne Collins, *Catching Fire*

6. Everyone is born with some special talent, and Eliza Sommers discovered early on that she had **two**: a good sense of smell and a good memory.

     Isabel Allende, *Daughter of Fortune*

7. She was surrounded by **children's things**: crib, toys, a dressing table, a little desk, and a bigger bed.

     Larry Weinberg, *Ghost Hotel*

8. I gave her **happy memories**: a ride on a merry-go-round, a kitten to play with, a special toy.

Lois Lowry, The Giver

9. **Animals** took shape: yellow giraffes, blue lions, pink antelopes, lilac panthers cavorting in crystal substance.

Ray Bradbury, "There Will Come Soft Rains"

10. I forced myself to turn, meaning to talk, but found myself instead looking over **her clothes**: her badly wrinkled skirt, her unpressed blouse tied in front like a halter so that every time she moved, a band of brown skin showed between blouse and skirt.

Rosa Guy, The Friends

WRONG COLONS

The colons below are incorrect because no complete sentence is to the left of the colons. (*Incorrect colons below should be removed because no punctuation is necessary.*)

EXAMPLES

1a. *Incorrect:* Homer enjoyed several activities, including: playing chess until late at night, watching the late show on TV, and munching on snacks during both.

1b. *Revised:* Homer enjoyed several activities, including these: playing chess until late at night, watching the late show on TV, and munching on snacks during both.

2a. *Incorrect:* Homer enjoyed: playing chess until late at night, watching the late show on TV, and munching on snacks during both.

2b. *Revised:* Homer enjoyed playing chess until late at night, watching the late show on TV, and munching on snacks during both.

3a. *Incorrect:* Homer enjoyed doing the same activities, such as: playing chess until late at night, watching the late show on TV, and munching on snacks during both.

3b. *Revised:* Homer enjoyed doing the same activities, such as playing chess until late at night, watching the late show on TV, and munching on snacks during both.

4a. *Incorrect:* Homer enjoyed every night doing the same activities, like: playing chess until late at night, watching the late show on TV, and munching on snacks during both.

4b. *Revised:* Homer enjoyed every night doing the same activities, like playing chess until late at night, watching the late show on TV, and munching on snacks during both.

5a. *Incorrect:* Homer enjoyed talking about: playing chess until late at night, watching the late show on TV, and munching on snacks during both.

5b. *Revised:* Homer enjoyed talking about playing chess until late at night, watching the late show on TV, and munching on snacks during both.

ACTIVITY 5

Match the list with the sentence that previews it. Write the result.

Sentence	List
1. He reminded me of the mummies at the Egyptian Museum: **^** . Mary Doria Russell, *Dreamers of the Day*	**a.** of the people, by the people, for the people
2. The barn was huge, and next to it were four small log buildings: **^** . Jeannette Walls, *Half Broke Horses*	**b.** upon the valance curtains of faded rose color; upon the rose-shaded lights; upon the dressing table; upon the delicate array of crystal backed with silver so tarnished that the monogram was obscured
3. He wished for all nationalities a nation like our own: **^** . Mary Doria Russell, *Dreamers of the Day*	**c.** fleshless, lipless, rigid
4. A thin, acrid pall as of the tomb seemed to lie everywhere upon this room decked and furnished as for a bridal: **^** . William Faulkner, "A Rose for Emily"	**d.** the granary and the smithy; the meat house, where hides and sides of beef were cured; and the poison house, which had shelves full of bottles containing medicines, potions, spirits, and solvents, all with corks or rags stuffed in their tops
5. Then the sounds of the forest returned: **^** . Michael Crichton, *Jurassic Park*	**e.** the first tentative croak of a tree frog, the buzz of one cicada, and then the full chorus

ACTIVITY 6

Create a sentence to preview the list, placing a colon between the sentence and the list. *Notice that items in the list are separated with commas (1–7 below), but if any one item is over ten words or already contains a comma (8–10 below), all items in the list are separated by semicolons.*

EXAMPLE

Incomplete: ^ a ride on a merry-go-round, a kitten to play with, a picnic.

Student Sample: **When my little sister started misbehaving, Mom would promise her anything to get her to stop:** a ride on a merry-go-round, a kitten to play with, a picnic.

Original: **I gave her happy memories:** a ride on a merry-go-round, a kitten to play with, a picnic.

Lois Lowry, The Giver

---

1. ^ : deep pity and wild exasperation.
Stephen King, Needful Things

2. ^ : a ring, a golden ring, a precious ring.
J. R. R. Tolkien, The Hobbit

3. ^ : a small bed, a tiny desk just large enough to hold a workstation monitor and keyboard.
Michael Crichton, Prey

4. ^ : the bedspread, the walls, even the ceiling.
J. K. Rowling, Harry Potter and the Chamber of Secrets

5. **^:** the horses, the wagon, the implements, and all the furniture from the house.

> John Steinbeck, *The Grapes of Wrath*

6. **^ :** a pheasant craning its neck to spy on us from a thicket, a crow hopping from branch to branch, a raccoon snoring in its den.

> Keith Donohue, *The Stolen Child*

7. **^ :** roast beef, roast chicken, pork chops and lamb chops, sausages, bacon and steak, boiled potatoes, fries, Yorkshire pudding, peas, carrots, gravy, ketchup, and, for some strange reason, peppermint humbugs.

> J. K. Rowling, *Harry Potter and the Sorcerer's Stone*

8. **^ :** a collar button and a piece of wool collar from the shirt he had been wearing when he was hit by the bullet; a shard of soft gray metal as big as a quarter; and, unaccountably, something that closely resembled a peach pit.

> Charles Frazier, *Cold Mountain*

9. **^ :** the shy willet, nesting in the ragged tide-wash behind me; the sand piper, running in little unfrightened steps down the shining beach rim ahead of me; the slowly flapping pelicans over my head, coasting down wind; the old gull, hunched up, grouchy, surveying the horizon.

> Anne Morrow Lindbergh, *Gift from the Sea*

10. **^ :** a few bookshelves and sporting trophies; a mantelpiece, crowded with greeting cards and signed photographs of boys and men; a worn oriental carpet; big easy-chairs; pictures on the wall of the Acropolis and the Forum.

> James Hilton, *Goodbye, Mr. Chips*

ACTIVITY 7

Create a list to attach to the sentence. Use a colon before the list, and separate the items in the list with commas.

Directions for 1–10: Make the items in your list under ten words each. Add the number of items indicated.

EXAMPLE

Incomplete: She had brought everything out on a tray: ^ . (*List five items on the tray.*)

Student Sample: She had brought everything out on a tray: **his daily vitamin tablet, a glass of freshly squeezed orange juice, a cup of coffee, some toast, and the newest copy of his favorite sports magazine.**

Original: She had brought everything out on a tray: **a pot of Darjeeling, the strainer, milk, sugar, and a plate of biscuits.**

Jhumpa Lahiri, *Unaccustomed Earth*

1. Everything is so broken: ^ . (*List three broken things.*)
   Mary Ann Shaffer and Annie Barrows,
   The Guernsey Literary and Potato Peel Pie Society

2. Something else is needed to get from sunup to sundown: ^ . (*List three things to help people who feel unloved get through the day.*)
   Toni Morrison, *Song of Solomon*

3. Our conversations centered around the kinds of subjects fifteen-year-olds talk about: ^ . (*List four things teenagers talk about.*)

> Keith Donohue, *The Stolen Child*

4. Shortly before midnight, he stepped on the plane at the Dallas airport, a tall, thin, balding man of thirty-five, dressed entirely in black: ^ . (*List four black items he was dressed in.*)

> Michael Crichton, *Jurassic Park*

5. The kitchen table was loaded with enough food to bury the family: ^ . (*List four foods on the kitchen table.*)

> Harper Lee, *To Kill a Mockingbird*

6. They were like the sounds heard in a dream you have again and again at certain critical turns of life: ^ . (*List descriptions of four troublesome dreams.*)

> Stephen King, *Just After Sunset*

7. Late strollers were still out: ^ . (*List six kinds of people strolling outside at night.*)

> Ray Bradbury, *The Martian Chronicles*

8. He befriended any number and species of animals: ^ . (*List six kinds of animals he liked.*)

> J. D. Salinger, "The Laughing Man"

9. The principles and practices of football and war are alike: ^ . (*List as many ways you can think of that football and war are alike. The original sentence has thirteen similarities.*)

> John McMurtry, "Kill 'Em! Crush 'Em! Eat 'Em Raw!"

10. From the room with the aquariums came smells: ^ . (*List as many smells you can think of that could come from a room filled with lots of aquariums. The original sentence has twenty.*)

John Steinbeck, *Cannery Row*

Directions for 11–20: Include in your list at least one long item (over ten words) or at least one item that already contains a comma. *Use semicolons, not commas, to separate the items.* (Whenever even one item is long or already contains a comma, semicolons instead of commas make reading the list easier.)

EXAMPLE

Incomplete: Abruptly there was color everywhere: ^ .

Student Sample: Abruptly there was color everywhere: **some neon signs aglow with vibrant fluorescent green, purple, orange, yellow and red; a flash of confetti-like fireworks over the center of Times Square in New York City, crowded with the typical New Year's Eve revelers assembled there every year; and hundreds of yellow taxis illuminated by the flashing signs and bursting fireworks to create a scene like a scene from a sci-fi update of the movie *The Wizard of Oz*.**

Original: Abruptly there was color everywhere: **the yellow streetcars and the sudden blues of telegraph boys jolting past with satchels full of joy and gloom; cab drivers lighting the red night-lamps at the backs of their hansoms; a large gilded lion crouching before the hat store across the street.**

Eric Larson, *The Devil in the White City*

11. He struggled clumsily for such a length of time that even my mind, shocked and slowed as it had been, was able to formulate two thoughts: ^ . (*List and describe two thoughts this person had.*)

John Knowles, A Separate Peace

12. In the beginning, in the evenings, his family went for drives, exploring their new environs bit by bit: ^ . (*List and describe three scenes the family saw during their evening drives.*)

Jhumpa Lahiri, The Namesake

13. They set three bowls of food before me: ^ . (*List and describe the food in the three bowls.*)

Keith Donohue, The Stolen Child

14. My mother believed in light, nourishing food for colds: ^ . (*List and describe three kinds of nourishing foods for colds.*)

Nancy Hale, "You Never Know"

15. The practice of speaking in front of his class allegedly overcame a variety of evils: ^ . (*List and describe four benefits for him in speaking in front of his class.*)

Harper Lee, To Kill a Mockingbird

16. Of course, there were things that bothered her: ^ . (*List and describe four things that bothered her.*)

Oscar Hijuelos, The Fourteen Sisters of Emilio Montez O'Brien

17. Under the lightning that flamed in the skies, everything below stood out in clear-cut and shadowless distinctness: ^ . (*List and describe six scenes lit by the lightning.*)

Mark Twain, The Adventures of Tom Sawyer

18. There are four kids: **^** . (*List and describe four kids.*)

    Barbara Kingsolver, *Pigs in Heaven*

19. Like most first-time authors, I was filled with hope and despair upon the book's publication: **^** . (*List the hope, beginning with these words: "hope that . . ." Then list the despair, beginning with these words: "despair that."*)

    Barack Obama, *Dreams from My Father*

20. They had all been so full of assumptions: **^** . (*List and describe four assumptions they had. Begin each with these words: "the assumption that . . ."*)

    Jhumpa Lahiri, *Unaccustomed Earth*

BEYOND THE PARAGRAPH

In his Pulitzer Prize–winning novel *Tinkers*, author Paul Harding has a sentence with a colon introducing a list of unusual accomplishments of an elderly man named Howard recalling events from his life:

> These are the things that Howard did at one time or another, sometimes to earn extra money, mostly not: shoot a rabid dog, deliver a baby, put out a fire, pull a rotten tooth, cut a man's hair, sell five gallons of home-made whiskey for a backwoods bootlegger named Pott, fish a drowned child from a creek.

Following that sentence, the author writes a paragraph for each of the seven events listed in the sentence, with details of each event. Here, for example, is one of the events—cutting a man's hair—narrated in just one paragraph.

EXAMPLE

> The man whose hair he cut was named Melish, *a nineteen-year-old due to be married in an hour and a half*. His mother was dead; his sisters and brothers, <u>all much older than he</u>, were married off already. His father was plowing their fifteen acres of potatoes and would have just as soon scalped the boy as cut his hair, because him getting married meant the last helping hands were abandoning the farm. Howard took a pair of shears and a medium-size tin pot from his wagon. He fitted the pot over the boy's head and cut in a circle around its circumference. When he was done, he took a hand mirror from its wrapping paper and gave it to the boy. The boy turned his head left and then right and handed the mirror back to Howard, **telling him it looked pretty smart**.

ASSIGNMENT

From that list of events Howard recalled, choose *three more events*, and then write a paragraph for each narrating the details of each of the three events.

The example paragraph above uses a semicolon once, and one identifier (an appositive *italicized*), one elaborator (an absolute <u>underlined</u>), and one describer (a participle **bolded**). To practice the sentence-composing tools and special punctuation marks you've learned, somewhere within your three paragraphs use at least once each of these:

SENTENCE-COMPOSING TOOLS

The Identifier (*appositive*)	pages 35–49
The Elaborator (*absolute*)	pages 50–66
The Describer (*participle*)	pages 67–84

PUNCTUATION MARKS

Having imagination, you take an hour to write a paragraph that if you were unimaginative would take one minute.

—Franklin Pierce Adams, *journalist*

BEST PARAGRAPHS

By studying how authors build their sentences, you practiced ways to improve your own sentences. You learned that "best sentences" are those with three parts: *a topic*, *a comment about that topic*, and *especially sentence-composing tools* like the ones authors use to build their sentences.

What are "best paragraphs"? Paragraphs have three similar parts: *a topic*, *lots of comments about that same topic spread across many sentences*, and *especially sentence-composing tools* like those used by authors.

In the paragraph below, the topic is this: a young woman named Ada attacked by a rooster. The comments about Ada and the rooster are spread across the eight-sentence paragraph. To illustrate the importance of sentence-composing tools within a paragraph, two versions of the paragraph are given below. In the first version, all of the sentence-composing tools are removed. In the second version, the author's tools are restored. Their restoration provides paragraph power.

PARAGRAPH WITHOUT SENTENCE-COMPOSING TOOLS

Ada waved her hands at the rooster. The rooster launched himself at her face. Ada was cut across the wrist by a spur. Her blow knocked the bird to the ground, but he rose and came at her again. The rooster dug at her with a spur. She burst from the bush with a great thrash and rose to run. The bird pecked at her calves and struck again and again with the spur of his free leg. Ada then ran to the porch and into the house.

In the next version, the author uses lots of tools. Some are familiar ones you learned earlier in this worktext—appositives, absolutes, participles. Other tools are new. All tools, though, are easy to identify because *all tools are removable sentence parts*. If a sentence part—familiar or new—is removable without destroying the basic sentence, it's a tool.

In this restored paragraph, focus on the power of the sentence-composing tools (underlined). Each sentence in the paragraph contains tools that add detail, meaning, variety, style, and texture to writing—hallmarks of good writing.

PARAGRAPH WITH SENTENCE-COMPOSING TOOLS

Trapped under the bush, Ada, shifting about onto her knees, waved her hands at the rooster, a black and gold menace that always frightened Ada a little with his ferocity. When she did, the rooster launched himself at her face, twisting in the air so that he arrived spurs first, wings flogging away. Throwing up a hand to fend him off, Ada was cut across the wrist by a spur. Her blow knocked the bird to the ground, but he rose and came at her again, wings fanning. As she scrambled crablike to get out from under the bush, the rooster dug at her with a spur, hanging it up in the folds of her skirt. She burst from the bush with a great thrash and rose to run, the rooster still attached to her skirt at knee level. The bird pecked at her calves and struck again and again with the spur of his free leg, beating at her with his wings. Ada, hitting at it with open-handed blows until it fell away, then ran to the porch and into the house.

Charles Frazier, *Cold Mountain*

Look at the paragraph's sentences side-by-side to see how tools make-over the paragraph. (*Sentence-composing tools are underlined.*)

1a. Ada waved her hands at the rooster.

1b. Trapped under the bush, Ada, shifting about onto her knees, waved her hands at the rooster, a black and gold menace that always frightened Ada a little with his ferocity.

2a. The rooster launched himself at her face.

2b. When she did, the rooster launched himself at her face, twisting in the air so that he arrived spurs first, wings flogging away.

3a. Ada was cut across the wrist by a spur.

3b. <u>Throwing up a hand to fend him off</u>, Ada was cut across the wrist by a spur.

4a. Her blow knocked the bird to the ground, but he rose and came at her again.

4b. Her blow knocked the bird to the ground, but he rose and came at her again, <u>wings fanning</u>.

5a. The rooster dug at her with a spur.

5b. <u>As she scrambled crablike to get out from under the bush</u>, the rooster dug at her with a spur, <u>hanging it up in the folds of her skirt</u>.

6a. She burst from the bush with a great thrash and rose to run.

6b. She burst from the bush with a great thrash and rose to run, <u>the rooster still attached to her skirt at knee level</u>.

7a. The bird pecked at her calves and struck again and again with the spur of his free leg.

7b. The bird pecked at her calves and struck again and again with the spur of his free leg, <u>beating at her with his wings</u>.

8a. Ada then ran to the porch and into the house.

8b. Ada, <u>hitting at it with open-handed blows until it fell away</u>, then ran to the porch and into the house.

THE NUMBERS

Sentences: Both paragraphs—the one without tools, and the one with tools—contain eight sentences.

Words: The paragraph without tools contains 88 words. The paragraph with tools contains 184 words, almost 50 percent more than the paragraph without tools.

Conclusion: Almost one-half of the content of the original paragraph comes from the author's use of sentence-composing tools.

The best way to write "best paragraphs" is to include within your paragraphs "best sentences." The best way to write "best sentences" is to use sentence-composing tools because they make just about anything you write, in high school and beyond, like the writing of authors.

---

*To condense the diffused light of a page of thought into the luminous flash of a single **sentence** is worthy to rank as a prize composition just by itself. Anybody can have ideas, but the difficulty is to express them without squandering a quire of paper [around 25 pages] on an idea that ought to be reduced to one glittering **paragraph**.*

—Mark Twain, author

SHOW ME HOW: PARAGRAPHS

Earlier, you learned to imitate sentences by authors. Imitating paragraphs by authors is similar. This section will show you how. Everyone knows that imitation is the sincerest form of flattery. After you finish the activities on sentence imitating, you'll see that it's also a great way to improve your writing.

ACTIVITY 1

Compare these four paragraphs to notice how the sentences in all four are built alike.

1. When you start smoking cigarettes, within a few months your body becomes physically addicted. Try not to start. Think about the damage to your body. Understand that smoking will be unhealthy, and when you smoke, you will experience coughing, yellow teeth, and breathlessness.

2. When a baby is conceived, in a little while the mother's body becomes radically changed. Let the change occur. Understand the process of birth. Know that the child will be born, and when it is born, you will have a beautiful, healthy, and wonderful baby.

3. When the clouds are full in the sky, over the hours the day appears depressingly long. Don't be gloomy. Make the most of this gray day. Believe that this day will soon be gone, and when it is gone, you will feel a rebirth of life, strength, and energy.

4. When you begin an exercise program, during the activities your body is continually challenged. Try not to give up. Avoid overtraining. Plan that your program will be gradual, and when you are ready, you will increase the frequency, duration, and intensity.

ACTIVITY 2

Write your own imitation of the same paragraph by building your sentences like those in that paragraph. First study the sentences, and then write your own imitation of each, one sentence at a time.

First Sentence: Jot down several ways these sentences are alike.

- When you start smoking cigarettes, within a few months your body becomes physically addicted.

- When a baby is conceived, in a little while the mother's body becomes radically changed.

- When the clouds are full in the sky, over the hours the day appears depressingly long.

- When you begin an exercise program, during the activities your body is continually challenged.

Second Sentence: Jot down several ways these sentences are alike.

- Try not to start.
- Let the change occur.
- Don't be gloomy.
- Try not to give up.

Third Sentence: Jot down several ways these sentences are alike.

- Think about the damage to your body.
- Understand the process of birth.
- Make the most of this gray day.
- Avoid overtraining.

Fourth Sentence: *Jot down several ways these sentences are alike.*

- Understand that smoking will be unhealthy, and when you smoke, you will experience coughing, yellow teeth, and breathlessness.

- Know that the baby will be born, and when it is born, you will have a beautiful, healthy, and wonderful baby.

- Believe that this day will soon be gone, and when it is gone, you will feel a rebirth of life, strength, and energy.

- Plan that your program will be gradual, and when you are ready, you will increase the frequency, duration, and intensity.

A paragraph is a collection of linked sentences. The paragraph below tells how a poor family assembled together in the kitchen after a terrible dust storm passed through their area. All of the sentences are linked because all of them are about the family's response to a storm.

MODEL PARAGRAPH

(1) Lying in their beds, the family heard the wind stop. (2) Slowly, they rose, wondering if the dust storm was over, murmuring their quiet questions. (3) They went down the upstairs hall, padding softly in their bare fee on the cold floor, heading towards the kitchen, the meeting ground for family conferences. (4) When they were all assembled, no one spoke to break the silence, a blanket on the night. (5) Looking toward their father, the source of strength, they waited, listening, hoping, praying that the calm outside would last.

John Steinbeck, *The Grapes of Wrath*

IMITATION PARAGRAPH

(1) Sitting at their desks, the students heard the alarm sound. (2) Quickly, they stood, wondering if the alarm was real, collecting their school things. (3) They went out the back door, hurrying in the early morning past the new construction, walking toward the parking lot, the assigned space for fire drills. (4) When students were all there, an assistant principal yelled the all-clear, an antidote for the alarm. (5) Glancing toward their teachers, the symbols of authority, they smiled, relaxing, chatting, knowing that the practice alarm was over.

ACTIVITY 3

Steinbeck's model paragraph is on the left, with an imitation of that paragraph on the right. Write your imitation of Steinbeck's paragraph, one sentence at a time. First study the sentence parts in the model and the imitation divided by slash marks. Then write sentences with similar sentence parts. As in the model paragraph, write your paragraph about any event lasting around fifteen minutes.

Model	Imitation
1. Lying in their beds, / the family heard the wind stop.	**1.** Sitting at their desks, / the students heard the alarm sound.
2. Slowly, / they rose, / wondering if the dust storm was over, / murmuring their quiet questions.	**2.** Quickly, / they stood, / wondering if the alarm was real, / collecting their school things.

3. They went down the upstairs hall, / padding softly in their bare feet on the cold floor, / heading towards the kitchen, / the meeting ground for family conferences.

3. They went out the back door, / hurrying in the early morning past the new construction, / walking toward the parking lot, / the assigned space for fire drills.

4. When they were all assembled, / no one spoke to break the silence, / a blanket on the night.

4. When the students were all there, / an assistant principal yelled the all-clear, / an antidote for the alarm.

5. Looking toward their father, / the source of strength, / they waited, / listening, / hoping, / praying that the calm outside would last.

5. Glancing toward their teachers, / the symbols of authority, / they smiled, / relaxing, / chatting, / knowing that the practice alarm was over.

USING IMITATING TO ENHANCE WRITING

WRITING PROCESS

Researching: The model paragraphs below are the opening paragraphs of stories. Imitate one of the model paragraphs as an opening paragraph for your true or fictional story.

MODELS: GREAT BEGINNING PARAGRAPHS

1. He rode into our valley in the summer of '89. I was a kid then, barely topping the backboard of father's old chuck-wagon. I was on the upper rail of our small corral, soaking in the later afternoon sun, when I saw him far down the road where it swung into the valley from the open plain beyond.

    Jack Schaefer, *Shane*

2.   He waited on the stoop until twilight, pretending to watch the sun melt into the dirty gray Harlem sky. Up and down the street transistor radios clicked on and hummed into the sour air. Men dragged out card tables, laughing. Cars cruised through the garbage and broken glass, older guys showing off their Friday night girls.

Robert Lipsyte, *The Contender*

3.   The driver of the wagon swaying through forest and swamp of the Ohio wilderness was a ragged girl of fourteen. Her mother they had buried near the Monongahela. The girl herself had heaped the grave with torn sods beside the river of the beautiful name. Her father lay shrinking with fever on the floor of the wagon-box, and about him played her brothers and sisters, dirty brats, tattered brats, hilarious brats.

Sinclair Lewis, *Arrowsmith*

4.   It happened that green and crazy summer when Frankie was twelve years old. This was the summer when for a long time she had not been a member. She belonged to no club and was a member of nothing in the world. Frankie had become an unjoined person who hung around in doorways, and she was afraid.

Carson McCullers, *The Member of the Wedding*

5.   When Augustus came out on the porch, the pigs were eating a rattlesnake, not a very big one. It had probably just been crawling around looking for shade when it ran into the pigs. They were having a fine tug-of-war with it, and its rattling days were over. The sow had it by the neck, and the shoat had the tail.

Larry McMurtry, *Lonesome Dove*

6.   This was a snail shell, round, full, and glossy as a horse chestnut. Comfortable and compact, it sat curled up like a cat in the hollow of my hand. Milky and opaque, it had the pinkish bloom of the sky on a summer evening, ripening to rain. On its smooth, symmetrical face was penciled with precision a perfect spiral, winding inward to the pinpoint center of the shell, the tiny dark core of the apex, the pupil of the eye. It stared at me, this mysterious single eye, and I stared back.

Ann Morrow Lindbergh, *Gift from the Sea*

Prewriting: Think about the situation described in your chosen model paragraph, and recall in your life or create in your imagination a similar situation that could begin your story.

Drafting: Draft the opening paragraph for your story, imitating each sentence in the model paragraph.

Peer responding and revising: Exchange your draft with other students in your class to get suggestions to make your paragraph better.

Creating a title: Create a title that hints at, but does not reveal, the topic of your paragraph.

I do a great deal of rewriting. With the beginning of a book, I will often rewrite first paragraphs, and the first few pages, thirty and forty times, because another belief I have is that in that moment, in those first crucial paragraphs and pages, all the readers' decisions are made.

—Brian Moore, *novelist*

BEYOND THE PARAGRAPH

The writer of the true story below, a student whose hobby is performing magic tricks, chose model paragraph 6 on page 147 to imitate to begin his story.

Later, he decided to finish his true story. Read it below to see how he used the three sentence-composing tools you learned earlier—the identifier (*appositive*—italicized below), the elaborator (<u>absolute</u>—underlined below), the describer (**participle**—bolded below).

Maybe you'll decide to finish your story, too, using, like the student below, the sentence-composing tools you've learned earlier.

Card Trick
by James Beltrani
(*a student paper*)

(1) They were his favorite deck of cards, smooth, flexible, and sturdy as the plastic cases of CDs. (2) **Stacked in a pile of 52**, the cards lay temporarily dormant, **waiting for their time of magic.** (3) Crimson red with snowy background, they were as beautiful and as delicate as a rose in full bloom. (4) On their smooth backs were drawn six angels, **resembling a cherubic collection of innocence**, <u>their faces an expression of enchantment</u>. (5) James gazed at that card deck, *a source of tricks*, and they awaited his magic touch. (6) *A novice magician, a sophomore in high school*, he nervously sat on a bench near the start of the boardwalk. (7) He stuck out like a sore thumb, **wearing pants and a collared shirt in the failing attempt to look professional, drawing subtle negative attention from half-dressed beach-goers passing by.** (8) He then anxiously paced a small area on the boardwalk while he fiddled with his cards, *a deck of red-backed Bicycle playing cards,* **gathering the courage to try his magic card trick with a stranger.**

(9) **Eyeing all the people who passed by**, he tried to find the best person to approach, *some trusting and trustworthy stranger to dazzle with card tricks.* (10) There was a large selection of people to choose from: *a*

young family taking their kids to the beach for some summer fun; a group of teenagers; an elderly man enjoying the view of the water and basking in the cool ocean spray from the waves colliding with the shore.

(11) "You can do this," he muttered to himself under his breath, **summoning courage to approach someone.**

(12) <u>His legs growing more unsteady with each nervous step toward his goal</u>, James, *teenage magician extraordinaire*, inched toward an old man who sat alone on a boardwalk bench, <u>a newspaper in his hands</u>.

(13) "You can do this," he repeated in a whisper. He hoped that repeating the phrase would make it true. He stood next to the old man, <u>his mind racing for the right words to say</u>.

(14) "Excuse me, sir," he said, <u>his voice wavering</u>.

(15) "Yes? What is it?" replied the old man, **annoyed at the interruption to his newspaper.**

(16) "I was hoping you could help me with something," the young magician replied. (17) **Extending his arms towards the stranger, fanning the deck of cards,** he waited for the old man to pick a card.

(18) The old man remained still, <u>his eyes scanning up</u>, <u>down</u>, <u>left</u>, <u>and right</u>, **trying to comprehend the young man's request.**

(19) "Pick a card, any card," James requested, **moving the deck of cards slightly closer to the man to make the card selection easier for him.**

(20) The old man remained still, <u>eyes still darting around</u>. (21) The magician stood patiently for what seemed like hours. (22) Finally, the man broke the tension, *an overwhelmingly awkward silence*. (23) He looked the magician in the eyes, grunted "Leave me alone, and go pick on somebody else," and darted his eyes back to his newspaper, **irritated that he might have missed something in the article he was reading**, *perhaps some gruesome detail of the latest suicide bombing, the latest stock market plunge, the latest hurricane devastation, the latest body count in some bloody war.*

(24) **Embarrassed, rebuffed**, the magician turned away, <u>his face flushed and reddening</u>. (25) He walked back to the boardwalk bench from where he had first spotted the old man, <u>his feet like lead weights</u>.

(26) <u>His spirit crushed</u>, he sat on the bench fantasizing about his magic card trick for someone who would never be so rude. His audience of one was himself—and, unseen, a little boy.

(27) After some time he felt a tentative tap on his shoulder. "Hey! From over there I saw you doing some card tricks. I was wondering if I could pick a card?" said the freckle-faced little kid, <u>a hesitant grin on his sunny face</u>.

(28) <u>An enormous smile breaking across his face</u>, James looked up, **reaching into his pocket for his cards, then fanning the deck of cards slowly between his hands for the kid to choose one.**

(29) With the card the little boy had selected returned to the deck, the magician performed a series of shuffles of the deck, **uttering in a forced deep voice mumbo-jumbo magic words to dazzle the kid**. (30) When the cards were thoroughly shuffled, he paused for a moment, smiled at the boy, cut the deck, picked up the card on top of the bottom half of the deck, and turned it right-side-up.

(31) "Is this your card?" he asked, **grinning**.

(32) "Wow! How did you do that?" replied the kid.

(33) "It's magic—and so are you!" James said. "Together, we made magic."

(34) They giggled.

IMITATING PARAGRAPHS

In this section, you will learn how the sentences in a model paragraph are built, and then imitate that model paragraph, using your own topic but building your sentences like those in the model paragraph.

PARAGRAPH DESCRIBING AN OBJECT

ACTIVITY 1

The model paragraph from Anne Morrow Lindbergh's *Gift from the Sea* describes a snail shell as she inspects it in her hand. Read the model paragraph and the three paragraphs underneath it. Which two paragraphs imitate the sentence structures in the model paragraph? Which doesn't?

To learn how the sentences in the model paragraph and the two imitation paragraphs are built alike, write out three equivalent sentences as a list: sentence number 1 from the model, plus the two sentences that imitate that sentence; sentence number 2 from the model, plus the two that imitate it, and so forth.

MODEL PARAGRAPH

(1) This is a snail shell, round, full, and glossy as a horse chestnut. (2) Comfortable and compact, it sits curled up like a cat in the hollow of my hand. (3) Milky and opaque, it has the pinkish bloom of the sky on a summer evening, ripening to rain. (4) On its smooth, symmetrical face is penciled with precision a perfect spiral, winding inward to the pinpoint center of the shell, the tiny dark core of the apex, the pupil of the eye. (5) It stares at me, this mysterious single eye, and I stare back.

Ann Morrow Lindbergh, *Gift from the Sea*

QUESTIONS TO ANALYZE THE MODEL

1. What sentence contains a simile (comparison)?

2. In sentence 4, what three phrases refer to the same part of the shell?

3. How do two of the sentences begin the same way?

4. How are the two main parts of sentence 5 alike?

PARAGRAPH ONE

(1) This is my room, dark, quiet, and at times lonely as a silent cave. (2) Small and private, it can absorb my thoughts like a sponge. (3) Safe and secure, it has a feeling of protection, providing a hiding place. (4) On its walls are displayed posters, reflecting interests of mine that have a huge range, a collection of wise sayings, an assortment of pop icons. (5) They elicit memories, those poster images, and I reminisce.

PARAGRAPH TWO

(1) Some rock stars are exciting to watch at live concerts, the fans cheering, the lights forming a kaleidoscope of color. (2) Thousands attend the concerts, which are usually held at large convention centers or outdoor theaters. (3) For weeks ahead of the concert, people get psyched, anticipating the special day when the concert hits town. (4) Despite what critics say, the behavior at concerts is loud, yes, but appropriate, with the great majority of people simply taking in the sights, the sounds, and overall ambience. (5) It's noisy, but nobody minds.

PARAGRAPH THREE

(1) That is a laser light, cool, ultraviolet, and invisible as air. (2) Precise and extraordinary, it gently reshapes the cornea by removing

microscopic amounts of tissue from the outer surface of the cornea. (3) Innovative but expensive, it is controlled by a computer, performing to heal. (4) Under the laser is sitting with anxiety a hopeful patient, focusing on the outcome of the laser eye surgery, a medical marvel of technology, a new procedure for glass-free eyesight. (5) It beams into the patient's eye, this machine with invisible rays, and the patient sits still.

ACTIVITY 2

Choose one of the sentences below—or create your own—to use as the first sentence of a five-sentence paragraph that imitates the model paragraph by Lindbergh (page 151).

1. That is an attic, musty, dark, and mysterious as fog.

2. This is a computer, sleek, compact, and fast as an electrical impulse.

3. Here is a baby, soft, warm, and pink as a rose.

4. That is the new car, shiny, stunning, and responsive as a racehorse.

5. This is a dandelion, feathery, light, and enchanting as fairy dust.

6. This is a marble, sparkling, colorful, and dazzling as a precious stone.

7. Here are the players, uniformed, determined, and coordinated as a well-oiled machine.

8. This is a tired eye, glassy, bloodshot, and unfocused as a bad camera shot.

ACTIVITY 3

The sentences from the model paragraph are broken down into their sentence parts to help you focus on how each part is built. Imitate each sentence part, one at a time, to write sentences for your paragraph resembling the sentences in the model paragraph.

1a. This is a snail shell,

1b. round, full, and glossy

1c. as a horse chestnut.

2a. Comfortable and compact,

2b. it sits curled up like a cat

2c. in the hollow of my hand.

3a. Milky and opaque,

3b. it has the pinkish bloom

3c. of the sky on a summer evening,

3d. ripening to rain.

4a. On its smooth, symmetrical face

4b. is penciled with precision a perfect spiral,

4c. winding inward to the pinpoint center of the shell,

4d. the tiny dark core of the apex,

4e. the pupil of the eye.

5a. It stares at me,

5b. this mysterious single eye,

5c. and I stare back.

ASSIGNMENT FOR A PARAGRAPH DESCRIBING AN OBJECT

Now that you have taken a close look at a paragraph imitation of an object (*snail shell*), choose a second real or imagined object to describe in another paragraph imitation.

Using the new model paragraph below, a description of a warehouse freezer, describe your object by imitating the sentences in the model. To simplify imitating its sentences, break each sentence down into a list of its parts, and then imitate one part at a time.

MODEL PARAGRAPH

(1) The freezer was a warehouse within a warehouse, a vast refrigerated chamber down at one end of the building behind a wall covered in sheets of galvanized metal studded with rivets. (2) A door, big as a barn's, covered in the same galvanized metal and battered as an old bucket, hung from a track. (3) It had been opened for the start of the shift, revealing a curtain of heavy-gauge vinyl clouded by oily smears and shales of ice. (4) The curtain had a slit up the middle so that the workmen could go in and out without too much of the cold air escaping. (5) The freezer was maintained at dead zero Fahrenheit. (6) Inside, there were no windows. (7) Stacks of cartons, tons of them, many of them packed with meat and fish, reached up three stories high on metal racks.

Tom Wolfe, *A Man in Full*

PARAGRAPH DESCRIBING A PLACE

ACTIVITY 4

The model paragraph from John Steinbeck's *Of Mice and Men* describes a bunk house on a ranch where migrant workers live. Read the model paragraph, and the three paragraphs underneath it. Which two paragraphs imitate the sentence structures in the model paragraph?

To learn how the sentences in the model paragraph and the two imitation paragraphs are built alike, write out three equivalent sentences as a list: sentence number 1 from the model, plus the two sentences that imitate that sentence; sentence number 2 from the model, plus the two that imitate it, and so forth.

MODEL PARAGRAPH

(1) Inside a long, rectangular building, the bunk house had whitewashed walls and an unpainted floor. (2) In three walls there were small, square windows, and in the fourth, a solid door with a wooden latch. (3) Against the walls were eight bunk beds, five of them made up with blankets, the other three unmade, exposing the burlap ticking on their mattresses. (4) Over each bunk there was nailed a wooden apple crate containing two wooden shelves for the personal possessions of the occupant of the bunk. (5) On these shelves were loaded little articles: soap, shaving cream, combs, brushes, razors, and medicines. (6) Near one wall there was a wood stove, its stovepipe going straight up through the ceiling. (7) In the middle of the room stood a big square table littered with playing cards, and around it were wooden apple boxes for the card players to sit on.

John Steinbeck, Of Mice and Men

QUESTIONS TO ANALYZE THE MODEL

1. What kind of phrase begins every sentence in the paragraph?

2. How is the content in sentences 4 and 5 related?

3. Which sentences reverse the usual subject/verb order by putting the verb *before* the subject rather than after it?

PARAGRAPH ONE

(1) At the end of a short, clean corridor, the classroom had colorful walls and a carpeted floor. (2) On three walls there were decorated bulletin boards, and on the fourth, a complete row of sparkling windows. (3) Inside the room were ten small desks, five of them equipped with paint boxes, the other five empty, showing the varnished wood on their surfaces. (4) Beside each desk there was located a small plastic crate containing several inside boxes for the school supplies of the occupant of the desk. (5) In these boxes were stored various items: pens, writing tablets, pencils, erasers, crayons, and stickers. (6) At the front of the room was a teacher's desk, its top covered with students' drawings. (7) At the side of the room was a large conference table filled with puzzle pieces and around it were more small chairs for the little children to sit on.

PARAGRAPH TWO

(1) Inside, finally, from the pouring rain, the two boys shook themselves dry, like dogs, onto the kitchen floor. (2) Mom came into the kitchen in the middle of the children spinning themselves, throwing raindrops all around, and was a bit upset. (3) The kitchen, she said, had just been cleaned and mopped that morning, but now the floor was wet and the counters splattered upon because of the arrival of the rain-soaked, muddy boys. (4) In the broom closet, the kids retrieved a mop, and went to work, drying the floor, with the oldest brother drying down the counter tops with a kitchen towel. (5) Like a prison guard watching every movement, Mom stood immediately outside the kitchen entrance, hands on her hips, a frown on her face, as they worked. (6) The brothers did their best to mop the floor, dry the counter, including all the canisters holding flour, coffee, sugar, and tea. (7) Gradually, Mom's frown started turning upside down, forming a slight smile, then broadening to a grin, while her two boys undid the kitchen damage from their muddy shoes.

PARAGRAPH THREE

(1) Beyond the outside mauve entrance door, the living room had cocoa walls and a hardwood floor. (2) On three walls there were comfortable, inviting sofas, and on the fourth, a brick fireplace with a brass door. (3) In the corners of the room were two desks, one of them made with a closed roll top, the other one left open, showing much paperwork on its surface. (4) On the corner of each desk there was standing a small decorative jar containing ample space for the miscellaneous needs of the owner of the desk. (5) In these jars were assorted desk items: stamps, return address labels, paper clips, pens, pencils, and staples. (6) Near one sofa there was a small table, its surface covered with artistic items. (7) In the middle of the floor lay a luxurious Persian rug decorated with intricate flowers, and around them were fascinating twining green vines for the room's inhabitants to study.

ACTIVITY 5

Choose one of the sentences below—or create your own—to use as the first sentence of a seven-sentence paragraph that imitates the model paragraph by Steinbeck (page 156).

1. Within the packed, messy bathroom cabinet, the shelves held outdated prescriptions and some empty bottles.

2. In the crowded Apple store, one computer showed blogs and some assorted pictures.

3. On the second floor of the dorm, my bedroom featured a neat desk but a messy closet.

4. At the teen heartthrob's concert, the audience contained swooning girls and some white-haired grandmoms.

5. During the half-time ceremonies, the football field held energetic cheerleaders and a tiger mascot.

6. Within the new technology wing, a huge classroom had rows of computers and the instructor's projector.

7. According to the morning traffic report, the interstate highway had an uncleared accident and very long backups.

8. On his calendar for the weekend's schoolwork, the assignments included two papers and a science project.

ACTIVITY 6

The sentences from the model paragraph are broken down into their sentence parts to help you focus on how each part is built. Imitate each sentence part, one at a time, to write sentences for your paragraph resembling the sentences in the model paragraph.

1a. Inside a long, rectangular building,

1b. the bunk house had whitewashed walls

1c. and an unpainted floor.

2a. In three walls

2b. there were small, square windows,

2c. and in the fourth,

2d. a solid door with a wooden latch.

3a. Against the walls were eight bunk beds,

3b. five of them made up with blankets,

3c. the other three unmade,

3d. exposing the burlap ticking on their mattresses.

4a. Over each bunk there was nailed a wooden apple crate,

4b. containing two wooden shelves

4c. for the personal possessions of the occupant of the bunk.

5a. On these shelves

5b. were loaded little articles:

5c. soap, shaving cream, combs, brushes, razors, and medicines.

> **Hint:** Colons often introduce lists. Use a colon to introduce your list of objects just as Steinbeck's fifth sentence does. (For more on colons, see pages 123–134.)

6a. Near one wall there was a wood stove,

6b. its stovepipe going straight up through the ceiling.

7a. In the middle of the room

7b. stood a big square table

7c. littered with playing cards,

7d. and around it were wooden apple boxes

7e. for the card players to sit on.

ASSIGNMENT FOR A PARAGRAPH DESCRIBING A PLACE

Now that you have taken a close look at a paragraph imitation of a place (*bunk house*), choose a second real or imagined place to describe in another paragraph imitation.

Using the new model paragraph (on page 161), a description of a family room, describe your place by imitating the sentences in the model. To simplify imitating its sentences, break each sentence down into a list of its parts, and then imitate one part at a time.

MODEL PARAGRAPH

(1) One wall of the family room is dominated by a brick fireplace. (2) The fireplace has a small recessed area that was built to facilitate indoor barbequing, though we never put it to use, chiefly because when we moved in, we were told that raccoons lived somewhere high in the chimney. (3) For many years the chimney sat dormant, until the day, about four years ago, that our father, possessed of the same odd sort of inspiration that had led him for many years to decorate the lamp next to the couch with rubber spiders and snakes, put a fish tank inside. (4) The fish tank, its size chosen by a wild guess, ended up fitting perfectly.

Dave Eggers, *A Heartbreaking Work of Staggering Genius*

PARAGRAPH DESCRIBING A PERSON

ACTIVITY 7

The model paragraph from Rebecca Skloot's *The Immortal Life of Henrietta Lacks* describes a picture of Henrietta, a woman who died young from cancer but whose body yielded an incredible medical breakthrough. Read the model paragraph, and the three paragraphs underneath it. Identify two paragraphs that imitate the sentence structures in the model paragraph.

To learn how the sentences in the model paragraph and the two imitation paragraphs are built alike, write out three equivalent sentences as a list: sentence number 1 from the model, plus the two sentences that imitate that sentence; sentence number 2 from the model, plus the two that imitate it, and so forth.

MODEL PARAGRAPH

(1) There's a photo on my wall of a woman I've never met, its left corner torn and patched together with tape. (2) She looks straight into the camera and smiles, hands on hips, dress suit neatly pressed, lips painted deep red. (3) It's the late 1940s, and she hasn't yet reached the age of thirty. (4) Her light brown skin is smooth, her eyes still young and playful, oblivious to the tumor growing inside her, a tumor that would leave her five children motherless and change the future of medicine. (5) No one knows who took that picture, but it's appeared hundreds of times in magazines and science textbooks, on blogs and laboratory walls. (6) She's simply called HeLa, the code name given to the world's first immortal human cells, which are her cells, removed from her cervix just months before she died. (7) Her real name is Henrietta Lacks.

Rebecca Skloot, *The Immortal Life of Henrietta Lacks*

QUESTIONS TO ANALYZE THE MODEL

1. How does each sentence begin—with its subject or something else?

2. How varied are the lengths of sentences in the paragraph?

3. Where are two identifier tools (*defined on page 35*)? Five elaborator tools (*defined on page 50*)? One describer tool (*defined on page 67*)?

4. How does the paragraph go from a physical description of Henrietta to her importance in science?

PARAGRAPH ONE

(1) Here's a photo in my scrapbook of a soldier I never knew, its outside edges untorn but fading with age. (2) He looks out at me and

smiles, uniform shorts sagging around his waist, bare skin completely exposed, body tanned deep brown. (3) It's World War II, and he hasn't yet reached the age of twenty-one. (4) His young unblemished face is handsome, his attitude energetically ambitious and serious, unaware of the marriage that is waiting for him, a marriage that would produce three daughters and impact the world of education. (5) A buddy on the Pacific Island of Saipan took that picture, and it has lasted seventy-some years in the scrapbook where it stays, within a sepia page and a worn book. (6) He is called John, the unremarkable name given to the remarkable family patriarch who was John's great-grandfather, born in pioneer days when courage and grit mattered. (7) People call him Johnny.

PARAGRAPH TWO

(1) On the desk is a picture, newly printed from the computer, with dazzling realistic color. (2) It shows my best friend acting silly, Waldo the Wimp, a nickname we gave him because, when we were kids, he was scared to jump off the high diving board. (3) Today, he's hardly a wimp, having been the star quarterback on Alexandria High School's team leading to district then state championships. (4) He still, though, calls himself by that nickname, even though his real name is Alfredo. (5) A good-natured guy, my best friend, he's been in my life ever since first grade, helped me through hard times, celebrated with me through good times, with the wisdom of a philosopher, the patience of a therapist, and the spirituality of a saint. (6) Now married with two kids, a boy and a girl, he honored me by making me his best man, and the godfather of his kids. (7) Friend is what I call him.

PARAGRAPH THREE

(1) There's a picture on my bookcase of the child I once was, the little girl waiting and watching with interest. (2) She looks at the pony

beside her and smiles, dimples in her cheeks, gingham shirt freshly ironed, sunshine catching her soft brown hair. (3) It's the early 1950s, and she has not reached the age of eight. (4) Her animated child's face is happy, her heart still young and innocent, ignorant of the future waiting before her, a future that would bring her more happiness and change the lives of students. (5) A professional photographer took the picture, and it almost appeared on the cover of a national riding magazine. (6) She's usually called Margaret, the name given to her by her parents, which was her grandmother's name, handed down from her mother's side several generations away. (7) Margaret's adult life is memorable.

ACTIVITY 8

Choose one of the sentences below—or create your own—to use as the first sentence of a seven-sentence paragraph that imitates the model paragraph by Skloot (page 162).

1. Here's a picture on my cell phone of a [*fill in the blank*] I admire tremendously, the close-up clear and vividly capturing [*his* or *her* or *their*] fine qualities.

2. That's a letter on my desk from an uncle I always loved, its handwriting wobbly and unclear from old age.

3. This is a web page bookmarked for return visits, its contents informative and authoritative about the details of the topic.

4. Here are ten video games on my shelf of fantasy stories I love, their boxes soiled and marred from repeated viewings.

5. There's a document on my doctor's wall from a medical school he obviously attended, its name featured prominently in large gold letters.

6. Here's a sketch in my notebook of a lovely old woman I just drew, its delicate and lovely minimalist lines capturing her profile.

7. That was an amazing concert at a giant arena where I had never been, its featured singer incredible and worshipped by adoring fans.

8. It was a difficult test from the teacher we all respected, its questions fair but challenging us throughout.

ACTIVITY 9

The sentences from the model paragraph are broken down into their sentence parts to help you focus on how each part is built. Imitate each sentence part, one at a time, to write sentences for your paragraph resembling the sentences in the model paragraph.

1a. There's a photo on my wall

1b. of a woman I've never met,

1c. its left corner torn and patched together with tape.

2a. She looks straight into the camera and smiles,

2b. hands on hips,

2c. dress suit neatly pressed,

2d. lips painted deep red.

3a. It's the late 1940s,

3b. and she hasn't yet reached the age of thirty.

4a. Her light brown skin is smooth,

4b. her eyes still young and playful,

4c. oblivious to the tumor growing inside her,

4d. a tumor that would leave her five children motherless

4e. and change the future of medicine.

5a. No one knows who took that picture,

5b. but it's appeared hundreds of times

5c. in magazines and science textbooks,

5d. on blogs and laboratory walls.

6a. She's simply called HeLa,

6b. the code name given to the world's first immortal human cells,

6c. which are her cells,

6d. removed from her cervix just months before she died.

7a. Her real name

7b. is Henrietta Lacks.

ASSIGNMENT FOR A PARAGRAPH DESCRIBING A PERSON

Now that you have taken a close look at a paragraph imitation of a person (*Henrietta Lacks*), choose a second real or imagined person to describe in another paragraph imitation.

Using the new model paragraph below, a description of Jim grooming himself, describe your person by imitating the sentences in the model. To simplify imitating its sentences, break each sentence down into a list of its parts, and then imitate one part at a time.

MODEL PARAGRAPH

(1) Jim stepped to the washstand in the corner and washed his hands and combed water through his hair with his fingers. (2) Looking into the mirror fastened across the corner of the room above the washstand, he peered into his own small grey eyes for a moment. (3) From an inside pocket he took a comb fitted with a pocket clip and combed

his straight brown hair, and parted it neatly on the side. (4) He wore a dark grey suit and a flannel shirt, open at the throat. (5) With a towel he dried the soap and dropped the thin bar into a paper bag that stood open on the bed. (6) A Gillette razor was in the bag, four pairs of new socks, and another grey flannel shirt. (7) He glanced about the room and then twisted the bag closed. (8) For a moment more he looked casually into the mirror, then turned out the light, and went out the door.

John Steinbeck, *In Dubious Battle*

ACTIVITY 10

In addition to description, writing often includes narration. A narrative is a real or imaginary story.

Written by recognizable authors, the model paragraphs below are the opening paragraphs of stories. Think of a story to write, but write just the opening paragraph of that story.

Study the model paragraphs below to learn how the authors attract the attention of readers, and then choose one model to imitate for the opening paragraph of your story.

MODEL PARAGRAPHS

1. I went back to the Devon school not long ago, and found it looking oddly newer than when I was a student there fifteen years before. It seemed more sedate than I remembered it, more perpendicular and strait-laced, with narrower windows and shinier woodwork, as though a coat of varnish had been put over everything for better preservation. But, of course, fifteen years before there had been a war going on. Perhaps the school wasn't as well kept in those days. Perhaps varnish, along with everything else, had gone to the war. I didn't exactly like this new glossy surface, because it made the school look like a museum, and that's exactly what it was to me, and

what I did not want it to be. I had always felt that the Devon School came into existence the day I entered it, was vibrantly real while I was a student there, and then blinked out like a candle the day I left. Now here it was after all, preserved by some considerate hand with varnish and wax.

John Knowles, A Separate Peace

2.   One minute it was Ohio winter, with doors closed, windows locked, the panes blind with frost, icicles fringing every roof, children skiing on slopes, housewives lumbering like great black bears in their furs along the icy streets. Suddenly, miraculously, a long wave of warmth crossed the small town, a flooding sea of hot air; it seemed as if someone had left a giant bakery door open. The heat pulsed among the cottages and bushes and children. The icicles dropped, shattering, to melt. The doors flew open. The windows flew up. The children worked off their wool clothes. The housewives shed their bear disguises. The snow dissolved and showed last summer's green lawns.

Ray Bradbury, The Martian Chronicles

3.   All he could see, in every direction, was water. It was June 23, 1943. Somewhere on the endless expanse of the Pacific Ocean Army Air Forces bombardier and Olympic runner Louie Zamperini lay across a small raft, drifting westward. Slumped alongside him was a sergeant, one of his plane's gunners. On a separate raft, tethered to the first, lay another crewman, a gash zigzagging across his forehead. Their bodies, burned by the sun and stained yellow from the raft dye, had winnowed down to skeletons. Sharks glided in lazy loops around them, dragging their backs along them, waiting.

Laura Hillenbrand, Unbroken

4.   For many years Henry Kitteridge was a pharmacist in the next town over, driving every morning on snowy roads, or rainy roads, or summertime roads, when the wild raspberries shot their new

growth in brambles along the last section of town before he turned off to where the wider road led to the pharmacy. Retired now, he still wakes early and remembers how mornings used to be his favorite, as though the world were his secret, his car tires rumbling softly beneath him and the light emerging through the early fog, the brief sight of the bay off to his right, then the pine trees, tall and slender, and almost always he rode with the window partly open because he loved the smell of the pines and the heavy salt air, and in the winter he loved the smell of the cold.

Elizabeth Strout, Oliver Kitteridge

5. The small boys came early to the hanging. It was still dark when the first three or four sidled out of the hovels, quiet as cats in their felt boots. A thin layer of fresh snow covered the little town like a coat of new paint, and theirs were the first footprints to blemish its perfect surface. They picked their way through the huddled wooden huts and along the streets of frozen mud to the silent marketplace, where the gallows stood waiting.

Ken Follett, The Pillars of the Earth

BEYOND THE PARAGRAPH

To apply what you've learned in this section, use one of the paragraphs you imitated from anywhere in this section as part of a longer piece of writing. Here are some possibilities: continue the story you began in Activity 10 on page 167, or use one of your imitation paragraphs for a different kind of paper in one of your classes, for example, an essay, a review, a report, or research paper.

Amanda's report (see next page), prepared for a science class, uses for her first paragraph her imitation of the snail shell model on page 151. Notice that the rest of her essay matches the quality of sentences she established in her imitation paragraph—but written without imitating.

Amanda uses abundant sentence-composing tools: identifiers (appositives) italicized (pp. 35–49); elaborators (absolutes) underlined (pp. 50–66); describers (participles) bolded (pp. 67–84). She also uses semicolons (pp. 116–122) and colons (pp. 123–134) highlighted in Amanda's report.

After studying how she uses those sentence-composing tools and semicolons and colons in her paragraphs, include those tools and punctuation marks in your longer paper.

Mitosis: The Dream of Every Body Cell
by Amanda Lo
(a student paper)

(1) It is a simple body cell, round, microscopic, and busy as a bumble bee. (2) Diligent and calm, it has a wish like every young child who looks into a wishing well. (3) **Determined**, it has the miraculous energy to change, **dividing into two new cells**. (4) Within its round, protective cell wall are stored securely with care the chromosomes, **floating inside the nucleus of the cell**. (5) It has a wish, *this small microscopic cell*, and its dream will come true. (6) Mitosis, *the process of cell division*, allows the cell to produce two new identical cells from the original cell through a long, structured process.

(7) For the cell to divide, it has to follow several steps in sequential order: *prophase*, *metaphase*, *anaphase*, *telophase*, and *cytokinesis*. (8) *The process where the cell prepares itself for cell division*, prophase contains several steps. (9) First, the chromosomes, *the part of the cell that holds the genetic material*, *the very long special string located in the center of the cell*, coils on itself like a thread bound together to form a thick rope. (10) This process allows the chromosomes to condense, **becoming held together tightly, reducing its surface area and volume**. (11) Then, the nuclear membrane, *the protective layer surrounding the chromosomes*, breaks down into smaller particles, <u>its constituents considered invisible in the cell because of its minuscule size</u>. (12) Finally, the spindle fibers, *the long rope-like structures*, **producing the appearance**

of the longitudinal lines stretching across a globe, form. (13) The spindle fibers are like strings held at the opposite ends of a cell. (14) Meanwhile, each chromosome attaches to a spindle fiber.

(15) After the cell completes prophase, it enters metaphase, *a process where the chromosomes move to the middle of the cell*. (16) Each spindle fiber, <u>its rope-like structure holding onto each chromosome</u>, **composed of small particles called microtubules**, *the small units that combine together and attach to a chromosome*, plays a tug-of-war game, *a routine game played during mitosis*. (17) The spindle fibers try to pull the chromosome toward its `pole; however`, the forces from each spindle fiber are of equal strength. (18) This causes the chromosomes on both ends of the pole to line up along the middle of the cell, **imitating soldiers standing in a straight line**. (19) After all the chromosomes line up, metaphase is completed.

(20) *The next phase*, anaphase, where chromosomes split in half, begins. (21) The spindle fibers complete another tug-of-war game. (22) However, in this process, the spindle fibers become aggressive. (23) **Becoming greedy, focused on winning the game**, each spindle fiber pulls its hardest on the chromosome, **using all its strength**. (24) This powerful force breaks the bond between the sister chromatids, *the term used to identify the halves of a chromosome*.

(25) The cell, **broken into two new chromosome pieces, finished completing anaphase**, enters a new phase called telophase. (26) In this phase, everything that happened in prophase is reversed. (27) This indicates that the spindle fibers break down into extremely small `particles; their` size is so small that they are considered to have disappeared within the cell. (28) The nuclear membrane, which was broken down during prophase, reunites its particles together to form a protective membrane around each of the newly separated chromatids. (29) <u>Each membrane fully developed</u>, the cell's chromosomes loosen up by unraveling back to their original state, <u>the chromosomes appearing like loose strings in the nuclear membrane</u>, **uncoiling from their tightly bounded rope-like structure**.

(30) Finally, the last step of cell division ends with cytokinesis, *the splitting of a cell*. (31) In cytokinesis, each nuclear membrane moves in opposite directions of the cell. (32) This movement causes the cell membranes, *the skin of a cell*, to split itself into two membranes; each membrane contains its own nuclear membrane and genetic material. (33) After this process is completed, the cells take a short rest and then repeat the same procedure again. (34) Therefore, cells are constantly replicating, **produced by undergoing the prophase, metaphase, anaphase, telophase, and cytokinesis in cell division**. (35) Because cells are the basic unit of life, mitosis replenishes the amount of cells in an animal or plant when the cells die.

(36) The cell's dream is straightforward and complex, yet it came true, **producing two new identical cells after it has completed the multi-step process of mitosis, which was a phenomena**. (37) The cell divided, <u>its chromosomes splitting apart as its spindle fibers pulled each half of the chromosome and separated them toward the opposite sides of the cell and a nuclear membrane broken down into miniscule particles during the process</u>. (38) The cell successfully fulfilled its wish, and it split into two new cells, **deteriorating its spindle fiber into simple, miniscule cell particles, reforming its nuclear membranes, containing genetic material in both newly formed cells, continuing to dream about replicating itself again,** <u>the dream sustaining the quantity of cells in a body,</u> <u>the endless process cycling again</u>.

I read my way [as a young boy] through approximately six tons of comic books, progressed to Tom Swift, then moved on to Jack London's bloodcurdling animal tales. At some point I began to write my own stories. Imitation precedes creation.

—Stephen King, *On Writing*

UNSCRAMBLING PARAGRAPHS

A reader cannot understand a scrambled sentence because the parts are out of order. A reader cannot understand a scrambled paragraph because the sentences are out of order. In the scrambled paragraph below, readers, confused, only know that the paragraph says something about a snake.

Scrambled Paragraph (sentence parts and sentences are out of order)

Were erect, which were truly like hypodermic needles, its two fangs. Was wide open the snake's huge mouth. Flicked in every direction its forked black tongue, bursting from a hissing sound from its throat. At the air bit it, and from the fangs of yellowish venom spurted great gouts.

Unscrambled Paragraph (sentence parts and sentences are in order)

The snake's huge mouth was wide open. Its two fangs, which were truly like hypodermic needles, were erect. It bit at the air, and great gouts of yellowish venom spurted from the fangs. Its forked black tongue flicked in every direction, a hissing sound bursting from its throat.

Tom Wolfe, *A Man in Full*

The two versions have exactly the same words, but the scrambled version is almost meaningless, a jumble of words, while the unscrambled version is meaningful, a collection of the snake's actions that readers can easily understand.

In good sentences, like those in the unscrambled version, sentence parts have a clear relationship to each other. In good paragraphs, sentences also have a clear relationship to each other. These activities focus on those clear relationships of sentence parts within sentences, and the sentences within paragraphs.

Zoom in now on how to achieve clear relationships within and among a paragraph's sentences.

Narrative Paragraph: A narrative tells either a true or a fictional story. Each list below, when unscrambled, will become one of the sentences in a narrative paragraph from Michael Crichton's *Jurassic Park*.

In Crichton's fictional paragraph, during a thunderstorm a tyrannosaur attacks a Land Cruiser (car) containing two children, a brother and sister.

Unscramble and punctuate the lists to produce five sentences. In each list, the sentence part that begins the sentence is capitalized.

Important: Type or write out the list of five unscrambled sentences from the activity below. In the next activity, you need that list to arrange the sentences into a paragraph that makes sense.

1a. with a muddy splash

1b. The rear of the car

1c. and then it thumped down

1d. into the air for a moment

1e. lifted up

2a. of the car

2b. The dinosaur moved

2c. around the side

3a. that blended with the thunder

3b. At the back

3c. a deep rumbling growl

3d. the animal snorted

4a. out of all the side windows

4b. The big raised tail

4c. blocked their view

5a. mounted on the back of the Land Cruiser

5b. and,

5c. It sank its jaws into the spare tire

5d. tore it away

5e. in a single head shake,

The five unscrambled sentences are not in a logical order that matches the original paragraph, so arrange them in a way that makes the most sense. Write out and punctuate the paragraph.

ASSIGNMENT FOR NARRATIVE PARAGRAPH

From an electronic or a print source, find an image showing action. Pretend that the action is part of a story you are writing, and narrate that action in a paragraph, zooming in so details are easy to see.

ACTIVITY 2

Informative Paragraph: An informative paragraph educates the reader on a particular topic. Each list below, when unscrambled, will become one of the sentences in a paragraph developed by examples from Richard Lederer's "English Is a Crazy Language."

In Lederer's paragraph, the contents prove that the English language is widely used and highly influential throughout the world.

Unscramble and punctuate the lists to produce the five sentences in the paragraph. In each list, the sentence part that begins the sentence is capitalized.

Important: Type or write out the list of five unscrambled sentences from the activity below. In the next activity, you need that list to arrange the sentences into a paragraph that makes sense.

1a. are made in English

1b. and the majority of international telephone calls

1c. are written in English

1d. Half of the world's books

2a. that English is a crazy language

2b. to face the fact

2c. Nonetheless, it is now time

3a. in the annals of the human race

3b. perhaps as many as two million words

3c. and has generated one of the noblest bodies of literature

3d. English has acquired the largest vocabulary of all the world's languages

4a. in the history of our planet

4b. English is the most widely spoken language

4c. around the globe

4d. used in some way by at least one out of every seven human beings

5a. is stored in English

5b. is written and addressed in English

5c. More than seventy percent of international mail

5d. and eighty percent of all computer text

The five unscrambled sentences are not in a logical order that matches the original paragraph, so arrange them in a way that makes the most sense. Write out and punctuate the paragraph.

ASSIGNMENT FOR INFORMATIVE PARAGRAPH

Write an informative paragraph about something strange that became popular: for example, a weird electronic device, a ridiculous game, a no-talent celebrity, a way-out book, a disgusting food, or something else. You may want to research your topic online before drafting your paragraph to learn more about why—against all odds—your topic is so popular. In your paragraph's last sentence, explain why the popularity of your topic is puzzling.

ACTIVITY 3

Process Paragraph: A process paragraph describes how something occurs or functions. Each list below, when unscrambled, will become one of the sentences in a process paragraph from Siddhartha Mukherjee's nonfiction book *The Emperor of All Maladies: A Biography of Cancer*.

In Mukherjee's paragraph, the contents show that the process of cell division, when abnormally distorted, leads to cancerous cell growth.

Unscramble and punctuate the lists to produce the six sentences in the paragraph. In each list, the sentence part that begins the sentence is capitalized.

Important: Type or write out the list of five unscrambled sentences from the activity below. In the next activity, you need that list to arrange the sentences into a paragraph that makes sense.

1a. more perfect versions

1b. of ourselves

1c. They are

2a. to live

2b. as organisms

2c. to grow, to adapt, to recover, to repair

2d. Cell division allows us

3a. to live at the cost of our living

3b. Distorted and unleashed, it allows cell cancers

3c. to grow, to flourish, to adapt, to recover, and to repair

4a. adapt better

4b. Cancer cells grow faster

5a. cell growth without barriers

5b. That this seemingly simple mechanism

5c. a testament to the unfathomable power of cell growth

5d. can cause the grotesque and multifaceted illness of cancer is

The five unscrambled sentences are not in a logical order that matches the original paragraph, so arrange them in a way that makes the most sense. Write out and punctuate the paragraph.

ASSIGNMENT FOR PROCESS PARAGRAPH

After selecting and researching a process online, write a paragraph describing how something occurs or functions. End your paragraph with a sentence that emphasizes the importance of the process you've described.

ACTIVITY 4

Memory Paragraph: A memory paragraph lists scenes from the past recalled by the writer. Each list below, when unscrambled, will become one of the sentences in a memory paragraph from Pat Conroy's *South of Broad*.

In Conroy's paragraph, the narrator is recalling fondly a football game against an obviously superior team during which his own team bonded strongly.

Unscramble and punctuate the lists to produce the six sentences in the paragraph. In each list, the sentence part that begins the sentence is capitalized.

Important: Type or write out the list of six unscrambled sentences from the activity below. In the next activity, you need that list to arrange the sentences into a paragraph that makes sense.

1a. for the rest of my life

1b. that I thought would last

1c. A bond formed between us and our teammates

2a. the whole night

2b. he and I defeated their running game

2c. Because we had worked out so hard during the summer

3a. one that happens all too infrequently

3b. It was a joyful and rapturous night

3c. in the brief transit of human life

4a. and, by the end of that game, loving each other

4b. slapping each other's helmets, pounding each other's shoulder pads, trusting each other

4c. We would jump up

5a. every play that either team ran

5b. I can remember everything about that night

5c. every block I missed or made, every tackle I was in on

6a. I fell in love

6b. as we fought against

6c. the strength of an infinitely superior team

6d. with the heart of my team

The six unscrambled sentences are not in a logical order that matches the original paragraph, so arrange them in a way that makes the most sense. Write out and punctuate the paragraph.

ASSIGNMENT FOR MEMORY PARAGRAPH

Write a memory paragraph about a special day or night in your life. Recall all of the actions and feelings that made it memorable. End your paragraph with a sentence that explains why that day or night will never fade from your memory.

ACTIVITY 5

Explanatory Paragraph: An explanatory paragraph explains an idea or fact, often through illustrations. Each list below, when unscrambled, will become one of the sentences in an explanatory paragraph from Stieg Larsson's *The Girl with the Dragon Tattoo.*

In Larson's paragraph, the sentences illustrate why a particular policeman is considered toughened by the crimes he's observed during his career.

Unscramble and punctuate the lists to produce the nine sentences in the paragraph. In each list, the sentence part that begins the sentence is capitalized.

Important: Type or write out the list of nine unscrambled sentences from the activity below. In the next activity, you need that list to arrange the sentences into a paragraph that makes sense.

1a. and took two years

1b. the assistance of the National Criminal Police

1c. Another required

2a. a hardened veteran

2b. was

2c. The policeman

3a. Two others

3b. within a few days

3c. were solved

4a. confessed to having killed his wife or brother or some other relative

4b. and, full of remorse,

4c. In five of these the murderer had called the police himself

5a. in which he had had to take into custody

5b. He would never forget his first case

5c. at an electrical substation

5d. before he caused others harm

5e. a violent and appallingly drunk worker

6a. he could look back

6b. upon an impressive career

6c. All in all

7a. he had brought in

7b. During his career

7c. poachers, wife beaters, con men, car thieves, drunk drivers, burglars, drug dealers, rapists, and one deranged bomber

8a. to the police's satisfaction

8b. The ninth case

8c. was solved

9a. in nine murders

9b. He had been involved

9c. or manslaughter cases

The nine unscrambled sentences are not in a logical order that matches the original paragraph, so arrange them in a way that makes the most sense. Write out and punctuate the paragraph.

ASSIGNMENT FOR EXPLANATORY PARAGRAPH

Write an explanatory paragraph about the accomplishments of a great person, someone you know personally—a friend, relative, colleague, and so forth—or someone in history, entertainment, sports, science, politics, religion, or another field. Describe the person's accomplishments throughout your paragraph, saving the most impressive accomplishment for last. Finish the paragraph with a sentence summarizing the greatness of that person's accomplishments.

---

*Proper words in proper places make
the true definition of style.*

—Jonathan Swift, *writer*

BUILDING PARAGRAPHS

Raw material is the basic material from which something is made: ingredients for a recipe, lumber for framing a house, material for clothing, and so forth. For paragraphs, the raw material is sentences. Just as raw materials like food ingredients, housing lumber, and clothing material can be assembled through the right processes into something good, sentences can also be assembled into something good—effective paragraphs. In this section, you'll work with "raw" sentences to transform them into well-built, stylish sentences, and then assemble them into strong paragraphs like those by authors.

ACTIVITY 1

Under each author's paragraph is a list of sentences from that paragraph. Under each author's sentence is the raw material for you to combine to imitate the way the author's model sentence is built. When you finish, you will have a paragraph with well-built sentences like the ones by the paragraph's author.

EXAMPLE

First Model Sentence from Paragraph One: Frankie's friends found themselves at the bottom of the canyon, thrown clear.

Raw Material to Combine to Imitate the Model Sentence:

a. Kowalski's partner found himself in the bottom of the boat.

b. The partner was still alive.

Result: Kowalski's partner found himself in the bottom of the boat, still alive.

PARAGRAPH ONE

(1) Frankie's friends found themselves at the bottom of the canyon, thrown clear. (2) The truck was near them, wheels facing skyward. (3) Struggling to the vehicle, the boys saw Frankie pinned under it. (4) They ran to the ranch house and notified the ranch foreman. (5) There was no hospital anywhere near Ridgewood. (6) The closest thing was the house of the town physician "Doc" Babcock, who kept a few spare beds to cope with the cuts and bruises suffered by the local loggers. (7) The foreman fetched Babcock, who rushed to the scene. (8) Babcock climbed through the wreckage and used what little medical equipment he had to try to revive Frankie. (9) When Frankie's parents arrived by special charter train from Des Moines, they were told that their son was dead, his skull and spine crushed.

Laura Hillenbrand, *Seabiscuit*

Model Sentence One: Frankie's friends found themselves at the bottom of the canyon, thrown clear. (*See example.*)

a. Kowalski's partner found himself in the bottom of the boat.

b. The partner was still alive.

Model Sentence Two: The truck was near them, wheels facing skyward.

a. The shark was circling them.

b. Its jaws were open wide.

Model Sentence Three: Struggling to the vehicle, the boys saw Frankie pinned under it.

a. The partner was reaching for the gun.

b. He saw Kowalski's corpse.

c. The dead body was clutching onto it.

Model Sentence Four: They ran to the ranch house and notified the ranch foreman.

a. He reached toward the body.

b. But he couldn't loosen the hand.

c. The hand was locked.

Model Sentence Five: There was no hospital anywhere near Ridgewood.

a. There was no help.

b. No help was anywhere near them.

Model Sentence Six: The closest thing was the house of the town physician "Doc" Babcock, who kept a few spare beds to cope with the cuts and bruises suffered by the local loggers.

a. The only hope was the chest.

b. The chest was the one with the sharp spears.

c. Those were the spears which could tear through flesh to injure with the power and pain.

d. The power and pain were delivered by the dangerous blades.

Model Sentence Seven: The foreman fetched Babcock, who rushed to the scene.

a. The partner found the chest.

b. It was the one which lay below the deck.

Model Sentence Eight: Babcock climbed through the wreckage and used what little medical equipment he had to try to revive Frankie.

a. The chest lifted through the hatch.

b. And the chest offered what little desperate hope he had.

c. The hope was to try to kill the shark.

Model Sentence Nine: When Frankie's parents arrived by special charter train from Des Moines, they were told that their son was dead, his skull and spine crushed.

a. When the boat shifted from waves under it, he was hopeful.

b. His hope was that the angle was good.

c. His strength was ready.

d. And his aim was ready.

PARAGRAPH TWO

(1) At night, lying on his infirmary cot, remnants of vodka and black bread tucked under his bed, Doctor Pan would escape to his own private planet, Ro, where an imaginary astronomer friend, Zi, had finally succeeded in building a machine to convert radiant sunlight into moral strength. (2) Using that machine to waft peace throughout the universe, Zi complained that it worked everywhere except on that restless spark, Planet Earth. (3) Doctor Pan and Zi debated whether Zi should destroy bloody, war-mongering Earth, Doctor Pan pleading for compassion given the planet's youth.

Diane Ackerman, *The Zookeeper's Wife*

Model Sentence One: At night, lying on his infirmary cot, remnants of vodka and black bread tucked under his bed, Doctor Pan would escape to his own private planet, Ro, where an imaginary astronomer friend, Zi, had finally succeeded in building a machine to convert radiant sunlight into moral strength.

a. It happened in sleep, curled on her canopied crib, samples of toys and stuffed animals scattered all around her body.

b. What happened was that little Louise would dream of her special place, Plantland.

c. Plantland was where a magical sheepdog friend, Poppy, had regularly participated in crossing a river.

d. Poppy crossed the river to save little girls from scary plants.

Model Sentence Two: Using that machine to waft peace throughout the universe, Zi complained that it worked everywhere except on that restless spark, Planet Earth.

a. Poppy was crossing that river to save small girls every night.

b. Poppy noticed that it flowed gently downstream.

c. It flowed gently except alongside the dark jungle, Fear.

Model Sentence Three: Doctor Pan and Zi debated whether Zi should destroy bloody, war-mongering Earth, Doctor Pan pleading for compassion given the planet's youth.

a. Little Louise and Poppy hoped that no one would ever enter that awful place.

b. The awful place was that frightening nightmare-producing jungle.

c. The jungle was called Fear.

d. Little Louise was shuddering in terror from that jungle's darkness.

PARAGRAPH THREE

(1) Among the most famous women to have lived, Cleopatra ruled Egypt for twenty-two years. (2) She lost a kingdom once, regained it, nearly lost it again, amassed an empire, lost it all. (3) A goddess as a child, a queen at eighteen, a celebrity soon thereafter, she was an object of speculation and veneration, gossip and legend, even in her own time. (4) At the height of her power, she controlled virtually the entire eastern Mediterranean coast, the last great kingdom of any Egyptian ruler.

Stacy Schiff, *Cleopatra: A Life*

Model Sentence One: Among the most famous women to have lived a royal existence, Cleopatra ruled Egypt for twenty-two years.

a. Among the most beloved cowboys to have ridden the cinematic range was this person.

b. John Wayne was this person.

c. He appeared on the screen.

d. He appeared there over forty years.

Model Sentence Two: She lost a kingdom once, regained it, nearly lost it again, amassed an empire, lost it all.

a. He played a cowboy once

b. He reprised it.

c. He always played it again.

d. He attracted a fan base.

e. He kept it always.

Model Sentence Three: A goddess as a child, a queen at eighteen, a celebrity soon thereafter, she was an object of speculation and veneration, gossip and legend, even in her own time.

a. He was a hero as a young man.

b. He was a presence on the screen.

c. He was a lifelong celebrity.

d. He was a source of admiration and envy.

e. He was also a source of imitation and derision.

f. He was all these things even in the infancy of movies.

Model Sentence Four: At the height of her power, she controlled virtually the entire eastern Mediterranean coast, the last great kingdom of any Egyptian ruler.

a. Something happened in the highlight of his career.

b. He played every conceivable kind of cowboy.

c. The cowboy was the final American symbol of rugged individualism.

ACTIVITY 2

Now, without imitating model sentences, combine each list of "raw" material to make one well-built sentence of a paragraph. The number of words in the original sentence is indicated. In your sentence, aim for approximately that number. Begin with the provided opening words from the original sentence.

As you near the end of this worktext, now is the time *to use all of the sentence-composing tools you've learned earlier* to combine these basic sentences into ones built like an author's.

PARAGRAPH ONE

A Bull Fight
from "The Undefeated"
by Ernest Hemingway

1a. Manuel waved his hand.

1b. Manuel was leaning against the *barrera* [barrier].

1c. Manuel was watching the bull.

1d. And the gypsy ran out.

1e. The gypsy was trailing his cape.

> Word count: 19
>
> Original sentence: Manuel, leaning against the *barrera*. . . .

2a. The bull pivoted.

2b. The bull was in full gallop.

2c. It pivoted and charged the cape.

2d. The bull's head was down.

2e. The bull's tail was rising.

> Word count: 16
>
> Original sentence: The bull, in full gallop. . . .

3a. The gypsy moved.

3b. The movement was a zigzag.

3c. And as he passed, the bull caught sight of him.

3d. The bull abandoned the cape.

3e. The reason for the abandonment was to charge the man.

> Word count: 24
>
> Original sentence: The gypsy moved in a zigzag, and. . . .

4a. The gypsy sprinted and vaulted the red fence.

4b. The red fence was of the *barrera*.

4c. As the gypsy sprinted and vaulted, the bull struck the fence.

4d. It was the red fence of the *barrera*.

4e. The bull struck it with his horns.

> Word count: 19
>
> Original sentence: The gypsy sprinted and. . . .

5a. The bull tossed into the fence with his horns.

5b. He tossed into it twice.

5c. He was banging into the wood.

5d. He was banging blindly.

> Word count: 12
>
> Original sentence: He tossed into it twice. . . .

PARAGRAPH TWO

A Snake
from "Far Away and Long Ago"
by W. H. Hudson

1a. A rustling sound came.

1b. The sound was slight.

1c. It came from near my feet.

> Word count: 9
>
> Original sentence: A slight rustling sound. . . .

2a. I was glancing down when I saw something.

2b. I saw the head and neck of a large black serpent.

2c. It was moving slowly past me.

> Word count: 17
>
> Original sentence: Glancing down. . . .

3a. Something happened in a moment or two.

3b. It was that the flat head was lost to sight.

3c. It was lost to sight among the close-growing weeds.

3d. But the long body continued moving slowly by.

3e. It was moving so slowly that it hardly appeared to move.

> Word count: 32
>
> Original sentence: In a moment or two. . . .

4a. Something happened because the creature must have been not less than six feet long.

4b. What happened because it was so long was that it took a very long time.

4c. It moved while I stood thrilled with terror.

4d. As it moved slowly, I was not daring to make the slightest movement.

4e. Also, I was gazing down upon it.

> Word count: 35
>
> Original sentence: Because the creature. . . .

5a. As it moved over the white ground, it had a strange appearance.

5b. It had the appearance of a coal-black current.

5c. The current was flowing past me.

5d. It was a current not of water or other liquid.

5e. But it was a current of quicksilver moving in a ropelike stream.

> Word count: 34
>
> Original sentence: As it moved. . . .

6a. Turning, I fled from the spot.

6b. As I fled I was thinking.

6c. I thought that never again would I venture into that spot.

6d. That spot was frightfully dangerous.

> Word count: 18
>
> Original sentence: Turning. . . .

PARAGRAPH THREE

Death of a Beautiful Red Bird
from "The Scarlet Ibis"
by James Hurst

1a. At that moment the bird moved.

1b. It began to flutter.

1c. But the wings moved strangely.

1d. The wings were uncoordinated.

> Word count: 13
>
> Original sentence: At that moment. . . .

2a. Something happened amid much flapping and a spray of flying feathers.

2b. What happened was that the bird tumbled down.

2c. It was bumping through the limbs of the tree.

2d. And it was landing at our feet with a thud.

> Word count: 28
>
> Original sentence: Amid much flapping. . . .

3a. Its long, graceful neck jerked twice.

3b. Its neck formed into an S.

3c. Its neck then straightened out.

3d. And then the bird was still.

> Word count: 17
>
> Original sentence: Its long, graceful neck. . . .

4a. A white veil came over the eyes.

4b. And then something happened to its beak.

4c. Its long white beak unhinged.

> Word count: 13
>
> Original sentence: A white veil. . . .

5a. Its legs were crossed.

5b. And its clawlike feet were delicately curved.

5c. Its feet were at rest.

> Word count: 13
>
> Original sentence: Its legs. . . .

6a. Even death did not mar its grace.

6b. It didn't mar its grace because it lay on the earth like a broken vase of flowers.

6c. The flowers were red.

6d. And we stood around it.

6e. We were awed by its beauty.

6f. Its beauty was exotic.

> Word count: 30
>
> Original sentence: Even death did not mar its grace. . . .

ACTIVITY 3

Unlike the last activity, in which sentence beginnings and breaks were provided, in this activity you will decide where to make sentence beginnings and breaks. Combine each list of raw material to make the well-built sentences of a paragraph. The number of sentences in the original paragraph is indicated. In your paragraph, aim for approximately that number. *Remember to use all of the sentence-composing tools you've learned earlier* to combine these basic sentences into ones built like an author's.

PARAGRAPH ONE

A Hunting Accident
from "The Interlopers"
by Saki
(Length of Original Paragraph: Five Sentences)

1. He found himself stretched on the ground.

2. One arm was beneath him.

3. It was numb.

4. The other arm was held almost as helplessly.

5. This arm was held in a tight tangle of forced branches.

6. Both legs were pinioned beneath the fallen tree.

7. His heavy shooting boots had saved his feet.

8. The boots had saved them from being crushed to pieces.

9. His fractures were not as serious as they might have been.

10. It was evident, however, that he could not move.

11. He could not move from his present position.

12. He could not move from there till someone came to release him.

13. The descending twigs had slashed his skin.

14. The skin was of his face.

15. He had to wink away some drops of blood from his eyelashes.

16. He had to do this before he could take in a general view.

17. The general view he saw was of disaster.

18. Someone lay near at his side.

19. He lay so near that under ordinary circumstances he could almost have touched him.

20. The someone was George.

21. George was alive.

22. George was struggling.

23. George was obviously, however, as helplessly pinioned down as himself.

24. All around them lay wreckage.

25. The wreckage was thick-strewn.

26. The wreckage was of splintered branches.

27. The wreckage was of broken twigs.

PARAGRAPH TWO

Falling Snow
from "The Dead"
by James Joyce
(Length of Original Paragraph: Seven Sentences)

1. A few light taps on the window pane made him turn to the window.

2. It had begun to snow.

3. The snow was happening again.

4. He watched it sleepily.

5. He watched the flakes.

6. The flakes were silver and dark.

7. They were falling slanted against the lamplight.

8. The snow was falling upon places.

9. It fell on every part of the dark central plain.

10. Also, it fell on the treeless hills.

11. It was also falling softly upon the Bog of Allen.

12. And, farther westward, the snow was softly falling.

13. There, it was falling into the dark ocean waves.

14. It was falling, too, upon every part of the lonely churchyard.

15. The churchyard was on the hill.

16. It was the hill where Michael Furey lay buried.

17. The snow there had thickly drifted.

18. It had drifted on the crooked crosses and headstones.

19. It had drifted on the spears of the little iron gate.

20. It had drifted on the barren thorns of plants.

21. His soul swooned slowly.

22. His soul also swooned as he heard the snow falling faintly through the universe.

23. And it also swooned as he heard it faintly falling upon all the living and the dead.

PARAGRAPH THREE

"An Old-Fashioned Victorian House"
from *The Martian Chronicles*
by Ray Bradbury
(Length of Original Paragraph: Four Sentences)

1. An iron deer stood outside.

2. It stood upon the lawn.

3. A Victorian house stood further up on the green.

4. The house was tall.

5. The house was brown.

6. The house was quiet in the sunlight.

7. The house was all covered with scrolls and rococo, with multi-colored windows.

8. Its windows were made of blue colored glass.

9. Its windows were made of pink colored glass.

10. Its windows were made of yellow colored glass.

11. Its windows were made of green colored glass.

12. Upon the porch were geraniums.

13. The geraniums were hairy.

14. Also upon the porch was a swing.

15. The swing was old.

16. The swing was hooked into the porch ceiling.

17. The swing now swung back and forth, back and forth.

18. The swinging occurred in a little breeze.

19. A cupola was at the summit of the house.

20. The cupola had diamond leaded-glass windows.

21. The cupola had a dunce-cap roof.

BEYOND THE PARAGRAPH

In the preceding activities, you combined "raw" sentences to make good sentences like those of authors. Now apply what you learned about building better paragraphs through combining sentences.

Below is a five-paragraph description about a homeless man in a seedy bar. Every sentence is "raw," most beginning in the same monotonous way: the subject. Revise by combining those sentences using sentence-composing tools you've already learned:

- identifiers (appositives) *italicized* (for review, see pp. 35–49)

- elaborators (absolutes) <u>underlined</u> (for review, see pp. 50–66)

- describers (participles) **bolded** (for review, see pp. 67–84).

Use those visual codes for the sentence-composing tools.

Note: In your revision you may add, change, or delete words.

PARAGRAPH ONE

The homeless man was still asleep. He was in the far corner. It was in a corner of the bar. He was snoring slightly. His head was back against the wall. The wall was a hard, concrete barrier. That barrier was between the man and the rest of the world. That concrete barrier scratched the back of his neck uncomfortably. That barrier was causing his skin to turn red with each restless move he made. Rats scurried amongst the corners of the room. They attempted to reclaim the areas this man had taken from them. Their noses were sniffing out the new smells he had brought in with him. Those smells were an unpleasant stench. They were the stench of a man living homeless. [*This paragraph has **124** words, with many wasted. Through combining sentences, reduce that number to make every word count.*]

PARAGRAPH TWO

The place was a bar frequented by seedy characters looking for cheap booze. It served as a haven for the man. It was a haven because it was a shelter direly needed. The need came with the sudden cold weather the city was experiencing. The snow was falling increasingly harder with the passing hour. The man felt safe there. He felt safe because it was a serene retreat. The room offered protection from the elements. The room also offered protection from the cruel people of the city streets. His face was pink from the cold. The man sighed in his sleep. The sleep was uneasy, disturbed. His breath was blowing out warm air. The warm air from his breath went into the chilly room. His limbs were twitching. The twitching came from his troubled dreams. [*This paragraph has **135** words, with many wasted. Through combining sentences, reduce that number to make every word count.*]

PARAGRAPH THREE

He had once been successful. He was a successful businessman. However, he had fallen onto hard times. Those were hard times which had forced him into bankruptcy. And they forced him into the streets. Something happened to him from living on the streets for the past five years. During that time his hands were scrounging through trash cans for bits of unused food. During that time, he had transformed from a handsome gentleman into something else. He had transformed from a handsome gentleman into a disheveled, unkempt wanderer from city to city. He was no longer recognizable. He was a wanderer, and his hands were begging for food or money. He begged wherever he went. [*This paragraph has **115** words, with many wasted. Through combining sentences, reduce that number to make every word count.*]

PARAGRAPH FOUR

Life had been hard on him. It was hard for him these past few years. His face had become wrinkled. And his face looked more like that of an old man than his actual thirty-five years. Now he turned over uncomfortably in his sleep. When he turned over, the hard floor was stabbing at the knots in his back. The bumps were digging in. All of this was causing him to squirm. It also made him unable to find a comfortable position to sleep in. He fondly remembered the days of his apartment. The apartment was luxurious. It was a lavish dwelling in the sky. It was a penthouse. It had a commanding view of the skyline. Its rooms were large and airy. Its appearance was clean and tidy. And it was interior-decorated. It was a sharp contrast to this seedy bar. [*This paragraph has **144** words, with many wasted. Through combining sentences, reduce that number to make every word count.*]

PARAGRAPH FIVE

He sighed and turned back over. He was pulling his blanket around him. The blanket was a ratty piece of cloth. He had found it in a trash can. As he pulled his blanket around him, his body was shivering in the cold January weather. This was what he had become. He was a bum. He was a former master of the universe of high finance. He was a person who wheeled and dealed from polished chrome-and-glass desks. He lived now in regret. His regret was deep, very deep. He was suddenly awake. He raised the bottle. From the bottle, he was gulping the rotgut wine. As he drank, he was hoping for a rush of warmth. There was a feeble smile on his face. The feeble smile happened as he sought liquored oblivion. [*This paragraph has **136** words, with many wasted. Through combining sentences, reduce that number to make every word count.*]

*That's the best part, **revision**. I didn't know in the beginning that I could go back and make it better, so I minded very much writing badly. Now I don't mind at all because there's that wonderful time in the future when I will make it better, when I can see better what I should have said and how to change it. I love that part!*

—Toni Morrison, *novelist*

PARTNERING WITH A PRO

Throughout *Paragraphs for High School: A Sentence-Composing Approach*, authors mentored you by modeling the kinds of sentences they use to build their paragraphs. You learned their sentence-composing tools for building your own paragraphs.

To improve paragraphs, often a good way is to expand them by adding sentence parts to sentences, and sentences to paragraphs. The result is elaboration, an essential quality of good writing.

Take a look at this basic sentence with just a subject and a verb—the minimum requirement to make a complete sentence:

BASIC SENTENCE

> The jury was ready.

Readers learn from that basic sentence very little, and want more.

EXPANDED SENTENCE (the addition is underlined)

> After forty-two hours of deliberations that followed seventy-one days of trial that included 530 hours of testimony from four dozen witnesses, the jury was ready.

Readers now get so much more information through the addition: specifically, all the time in hours and days involved in deliberations and testimony necessary for the jury to give its verdict.

FURTHER EXPANDED SENTENCE (additions are underlined)

> After forty-two hours of deliberations that followed seventy-one days of trial that included 530 hours of testimony from four dozen witnesses, and after a lifetime of sitting silently as the lawyers haggled and the judge lectured and the spectators watched like hawks for telltale signs, the jury was ready.

This version is the original sentence by John Grisham from his novel *The Appeal*. Readers now get the full picture, including the time it took before the jury reached its verdict, plus the activities the jury observed involving lawyers, spectators, and the judge.

Here are two versions of paragraphs in which that sentence appears. The first version, the basic paragraph, contains stripped-down sentences like the one above. The second version, the original paragraph the author wrote, contains expanded sentences. (Additions are underlined.)

BASIC PARAGRAPH

The jury was ready. Ten of them proudly signed their names to the verdict. There were hugs and smiles and no small measure of self-congratulation. (**3 sentences, 25 words**)

EXPANDED PARAGRAPH

After forty-two hours of deliberations that followed seventy-one days of trial that included 530 hours of testimony from four dozen witnesses, and after a lifetime of sitting silently as the lawyers haggled and the judge lectured and the spectators watched like hawks for telltale signs, the jury was ready. Locked away in the jury room, secluded and secure, ten of them proudly signed their names to the verdict, while the other two pouted in their corners, detached and miserable in their dissension. There were hugs and smiles and no small measure of self-congratulation, all because they had survived this little war and could now march proudly back into the arena with a decision, a verdict they had rescued through sheer determination and the dogged pursuit of compromise. (**3 sentences, 127 words—5 times the number of the basic paragraph**)

The best cars have lots of extras to attract buyers, accessories like great sound systems, stunning wheels, leather seats, and so forth. The best paragraphs, and the sentences they contain, also have extras to attract readers, sentence parts and sentences that add useful details and information. Accessories are to cars what elaboration is to writing: namely, a much better product.

Now, prepare for a challenge: you and a professional writer (a "pro") will partner to compose paragraphs, the pro contributing some of the writing, and you the rest. The pro contributes the topic, plus a few sentences for that paragraph—but stripped down to the basics; you contribute sentence parts that will make the paragraph worthy of the pro. In short, your challenge is to write on the same high level as the authors whose sentences and paragraphs appear throughout this worktext.

In the following activities, with the help of pro partners, you'll practice expanding sentences and paragraphs by adding more information so that your writing goes beyond the basics to become more like an author's.

Your accountability partner keeps you on track and moving forward in all aspects of your development.

—Mike Staver, *motivational author*

ACTIVITY 1

Pros know this: additions make better paragraphs. Underneath each summary is a list of sentences (and below them, additions) that appear in the original pro paragraph. Insert the additions where they are most effective, punctuating them with commas where needed. Notice how the additions increase the interest of the paragraph.

PARAGRAPH ONE (from "The Scarlet Ibis" by James Hurst)

A young boy named Doodle is broken-hearted at the death of a beautiful bird, a scarlet ibis. Like many children whose pet dies, he wants to show his love for the bird by giving it a decent burial. In this paragraph, while Doodle's family watches him from a window in his house, Doodle buries the bird.

Note: *The additions are scrambled, not in the order they appear in the original sentence. Insert them where they make the most sense.*

1. Doodle took out a piece of string from his pocket, and looped one end around its neck.

    a. without touching the ibis

    b. gently

    c. dead near him on the ground

2. He carried the bird around to the front yard and dug a hole in the flower garden.

    a. next to the petunia bed

    b. slowly

    c. while singing softly "Shall We Gather at the River"

3. We were watching him, but he didn't know it.

    a. in amazement

    b. through the front window

4. His awkwardness at digging the hole made us laugh, and we covered our mouths so he wouldn't hear.

    a. out of respect

    b. whose handle was twice as long as he was

    c. with the shovel

    d. with our hand

5. We were at the table.

    a. seriously eating our cobbler

    b. when Doodle came into the dining room

6. He was pale.

    a. lingering just inside the screen door

    b. sad

7. "Did you get the scarlet ibis buried?" asked Daddy.

8. Doodle didn't speak.

    a. nodding his head

    b. eyes downcast

PARAGRAPH TWO (from *To Kill a Mockingbird* by Harper Lee)

This is a slight adaptation of the first paragraph in the novel, a preview of the entire story in just a few sentences. It mentions the injury to Jem's arm, and the rest of the story leads up to how his arm got broken—and why. After readers finish the novel, they can reread this paragraph and only then fully understand it.

Note: *The additions are scrambled, not in the order they appear in the original sentence. Insert them where they make the most sense.*

1. My brother Jem got his arm badly broken at the elbow.

    a. who was four years my senior

    b. when he was thirteen

2. He was seldom self-conscious about his injury.

   a. and when Jem's fears of never being able to play football were assuaged

   b. when it healed

3. His left arm was somewhat shorter than his right.

4. The back of his hand was at right angles to his body.

   a. his thumb parallel to his thigh

   b. when he stood or walked

5. He couldn't have cared less.

   a. so long as he could still pass and punt

   b. actually

6. We sometimes discussed the events leading to his accident.

   a. enabling us to look back on them

   b. when enough years had gone by

PARAGRAPH THREE (from *The Stand* by Stephen King)

A character named Harold, pondering over what course of action to take, feels drawn toward his decision, much like a slug (a small piece of metal) is drawn toward a magnet. As if compelled by external forces, Harold imagines a comparison between himself and the slug, both unable to resist the inevitable. Author Stephen King describes it this way: "Harold had felt that process begin in himself. He was the steel slug just that distance from the magnet where a little push sends it farther than the force imparted would do under more ordinary circumstances. He could feel the jittering in himself."

Note: *The additions are scrambled, not in the order they appear in the original sentence. Insert them where they make the most sense.*

1. Nothing happens.

   a. and if you put a steel slug on the other end

   b. if you put a magnet on one end of a table

2. A time will come when the shove you give the slug seems to propel it farther than it should.

   a. in slow increments of distance

   b. if you move the slug closer to the magnet

3. The slug stops.

   a. as though part of its liveliness is a resentment of the physical law that deals with inertia

   b. as if it has come alive

   c. but reluctantly

4. Another little push or two and you can almost see the slug trembling on the table.

   a. seeming to jitter and vibrate slightly

   b. or perhaps even actually

   c. the ones which look like knuckle-sized knots of wood but which actually have a live worm inside

   d. like one of those Mexican jumping beans you can buy in novelty shops

5. The slug moves on its own.

   a. faster and faster

   b. until it finally smacks into the magnet and sticks there

   c. wholly alive now

PARAGRAPH FOUR (from *The Grapes of Wrath* by John Steinbeck)

Near the end of this novel, a torrential rain causes rising streams to overflow, flooding the area where poverty-stricken migrant workers and their families had set up their tents: "The muddy water whirled along the bank sides of streams until at last it spilled over into the fields of the tents of the workers, which became lakes filled with tents." The paragraph below, based upon Steinbeck's description of the flood, shows the migrant families being forced by rising flood waters to abandon those tents to seek higher ground and shelter in a barn.

Note: *The additions are scrambled, not in the order they appear in the original sentence. Insert them where they make the most sense.*

1. The migrant people huddled in their tents.

    a. fearing the rising waters around their tents

    b. when the first rain started

    c. wondering how long the rains would last

2. The men built little dikes around the tents.

    a. out in the rain with shovels

    b. when puddles formed there

3. The beating rain worked at the canvas.

    a. the little dikes quickly washing out

    b. sending streams down

    c. until it penetrated

4. The water and the streams wet the beds and the blankets.

   a. the people sitting in wet clothes

   b. coming inside

5. They put up boxes.

   a. laying planks atop them

   b. in desperation

6. They sat on the planks.

   a. then

   b. day and night

7. Their old cars stood.

   a. water fouling the ignition wires and carburetors

   b. beside the tents

8. The people waded away.
   a. seeking higher ground

   b. cars useless

   c. carrying their wet blankets in their arms

9. They splashed along.
   a. carrying the very old

   b. in their arms

   c. carrying the children

PARAGRAPH FIVE (from *In Cold Blood* by Truman Capote)

This nonfiction book recounts in vivid, terrifying detail the killings of an innocent family on their small farm in a tiny Kansas village. The murders shocked the townspeople, replaced peace and friendliness among them with mutual fear and suspicion. The aftermath of the killings revealed how gentle lives and mutual trust were shattered by remembered gunshots in the middle of one tragic night.

Note: *The additions are scrambled, not in the order they appear in the original sentence. Insert them where they make the most sense.*

1. Few Americans had ever heard of the village of Holcomb, Kansas.

   a. in fact, few Kansans

   b. until one morning in mid-November of 1959

2. Drama had never happened there.

   a. in the shape of exceptional happenings

   b. like the motorists on the highway

   c. like the yellow trains streaking down the Santa Fe tracks

   d. like the waters of the river

3. The inhabitants of the village were satisfied that this fact should be so.

   a. to work, to hunt, to watch television, to attend school socials, choir practice, meetings of the 4-H Club

   b. numbering two hundred and seventy

   c. quite content to exist inside ordinary life

4. Certain foreign sounds impinged on the nightly normal Holcomb noises, on the keening hysteria of coyotes, the dry scrape of scuttling tumbleweed, the racing receding wail of locomotive whistles.

   a. a Sunday morning

   b. but then

   c. on the earliest hours of that November morning

5. Not a soul in sleeping Holcomb heard them.

   a. four shotgun blasts that all told ended four human lives

   b. at the time

6. The townspeople found fantasy recreating those shotgun blasts over and over again.

   a. afterward

   b. those somber explosions that stimulated fires of mistrust in the glare of which many old neighbors viewed each other strangely

   c. and as strangers

   d. theretofore sufficiently unfearful of each other to seldom trouble to lock their doors

ACTIVITY 2

In the paragraphs below, the pro's additions have been removed. Your job, as the pro's partner, is to add sentence parts to elevate the content and style to produce a paragraph worthy of a pro. The number of words in both the basic paragraph and in the original paragraph is provided. Through your additions, try to approximate the number of words in the original paragraph.

EXAMPLE

Topic: Three Men Witnessing a Hanging

At a hanging of a man during the fourteenth-century in Europe, three men are described in detail: a knight, a monk, and a priest.

adapted from *The Pillars of the Earth* by Ken Follett

Basic Paragraph

(1) The knight was clearly a person of some importance. (2) The monk was much older. (3) Most striking was the priest.

Original Paragraph (*the authors' additions are in bold*)

(1) The knight, **a fleshy man with yellow hair,** was clearly a person of some importance, **for he rode a war-horse, a huge beast that cost as much as a carpenter earned in ten years.** (2) The monk was much older, **perhaps fifty or more, a tall, thin man who sat slumped in his saddle as if life were a wearisome burden to him.** (3) Most striking was the priest, **a young man with a sharp nose and lank black hair, wearing black robes and riding a chestnut stallion.**

Note: *The basic paragraph has 19 words; the original paragraph 86 words,* **with more than 75 percent of the original being additions.**

PARAGRAPH ONE: A LIVE RAT EATEN BY A TIGER ON A RAFT

Lost and adrift at sea, a young boy named Pi, the story's narrator, is alone on a large raft—except for the presence of a ferocious tiger. Previously in hiding, a rat suddenly appears, alarming the boy and surprising the tiger.

Yann Martel, *The Life of Pi* (adapted)

Basic Paragraph

(1) A scrawny brown rat materialized on the side bench. (2) The tiger looked as astonished as I was. (3) The rat leapt onto the tarpaulin and raced my way. (4) My legs gave way beneath me. (5) The rodent hopped over the various parts of the raft, jumped onto me, and climbed to the top of my head. (6) I grabbed the rat and threw it to the tiger. (7) I can still see it as it sailed through the air. (8) The tiger opened its maw, and the squealing rat disappeared into it. (9) Its hairless tail vanished.

Note: *The basic paragraph has 91 words; the original paragraph 158 words, **with almost 35 percent of the original being additions**.*

PARAGRAPH TWO: SPIDERS ATTACKING A PROWLER

In this terrifying incident, a prowler at night attempts to enter a house through an opening in a window. The mother and her three children awaken, defenseless, until the children release on the intruder's body black widow spiders they keep as pets in several glass jars.

Pat Conroy, *The Prince of Tides* (adapted)

Basic Paragraph

(1) We saw his huge leg swing into the window. (2) Luke opened four jars of black widows and emptied them on his trouser leg. (3) The man's other leg slid through the window. (4) The first black widow sent her venom shooting through his bloodstream. (5) We saw those huge legs withdraw from the window. (6) The spiders were in the folds and creases of his trousers. (7) He felt them moving on him, and he rolled down the roof. (8) We heard his body hit the ground outside the window. (9) He was screaming now.

Note: *The basic paragraph has 88 words; the original paragraph 145 words, **with almost 40 percent of the original being additions**.*

PARAGRAPH THREE: AN APPROACH OF A DINOSAUR

A dinosaur appears suddenly on the horizon. In this paragraph, the vivid, detailed description of a dinosaur's body parts show an image of a huge, menacing beast.

Ray Bradbury, "The Sound of Thunder" (adapted)

Basic Paragraph

(1) The dinosaur came on great oiled, resilient, striding legs. (2) It towered thirty feet above half of the trees. (3) Each lower leg was a piston. (4) Each thigh was a ton of meat, ivory, and steel mesh. (5) From the great breathing cage of the upper body those two delicate arms dangled out front. (6) The head itself lifted easily upon the sky. (7) Its mouth gaped. (8) Its eyes rolled. (9) It closed its mouth in a death grin. (10) It ran.

Note: *The basic paragraph has 75 words; the original paragraph 179 words, **with almost 60 percent of the original being additions**.*

TOPIC: A MANSION NEAR A BEACH

The narrator visits some acquaintances who live in an expensive large house on a beach of a bay. This paragraph is the narrator's description of the elegant and luxurious details of the exterior of the mansion.

F. Scott Fitzgerald, *The Great Gatsby* (adapted)

Basic Paragraph

(1) I drove over to see some friends. (2) Their lawn started at the beach and ran toward the front door for a quarter of a mile. (3) Their house was even more elaborate than I expected. (4) The front of the house was broken by a line of French windows.

Note: *The basic paragraph has 47 words; the original paragraph 114 words, **with almost 60 percent of the original being additions**.*

PARAGRAPH FIVE: EIGHTY-YARD RUN FOR A TOUCHDOWN

A football player catches a pass downfield, and then makes an amazing run to the goal line to score a touchdown, dodging various members of the defensive team trying to stop him.

Irwin Shaw, "The Eighty-Yard Run" (adapted)

Basic Paragraph

(1) The pass was high and wide and he jumped for it. (2) The center floated by. (3) He had ten yards in the clear and picked up speed. (4) He smiled a little to himself as he ran. (5) The first halfback came at him. (6) There was only the safety man now. (7) He tucked the ball in. (8) He was sure he was going to get past the safety man. (9) He headed right for the safety man. (10) He pivoted away keeping his arm locked.

Note: *The basic paragraph has 79 words; the original paragraph 295 words,* **with almost 80 percent of the original being additions.**

ACTIVITY 3

Now, go solo, inspired but not directed by a pro. Think of books you have read—either on your own, like one of the Harry Potter or Twilight series, or for school, like *To Kill a Mockingbird* or the *Lord of the Flies* (or one from the list below). Then write two paragraphs about the event for one of those books. Choose either a retelling of an event already in the story, or a creation of a new event for a sequel to the book.

Paragraph One: As in the example below, write one paragraph setting the scene so your readers will know where in the book (or its sequel) the event occurs.

Paragraph Two: Draft, revise, finalize, and publish one paragraph that retells an event from that book (or creates an event for its sequel). Give this paragraph a creative title.

This time without help from a pro, make all the decisions for the paragraph yourself: what to say, how much to say, and how to say it—but make it interesting, even memorable.

Below are two examples: a paragraph retelling an event from John Steinbeck's *Of Mice and Men*; and a paragraph creating an event for a sequel to William Golding's *Lord of the Flies*.

Regardless of which you choose for your book—a retold event or a created event—your goal is not to match the style of the author but to write a paragraph demonstrating what you've learned in *Paragraphs for High School: A Sentence-Composing Approach*.

EXAMPLE OF A RETOLD EVENT

Paragraph One: *Setting the Scene*

(1) In John Steinbeck's *Of Mice and Men*, the main characters George and Lennie are very different in size of body and sharpness of mind. (2) George, of average size and normal intelligence, is the caretaker of Lennie, of huge size and low intelligence. (3) The paragraph below retells the incident where Lennie, a strong man with a childlike mind and heart but the body of a giant, reluctantly fights Curley, a mean little guy who picked a fight with Lennie. (4) Curley starts cruelly hitting the innocent Lennie, but Lennie, fearful that George standing by will disapprove, doesn't fight back. (5) However, when Curley draws blood from Lennie, repeatedly pounding him with his fists, George finally yells to Lennie, "Get 'em, Lennie!" (6) Lennie then grabs Curley's fist in midair, clenching and squeezing it until it's pulverized.

Paragraph Two: *Describing the Scene*

The Gentle Pulverizer

(1) Afraid to fight back when Curley attacked him, not because of fear of Curley but because of fear that George wouldn't approve and

would scold him for fighting, Lennie withstood the brutal attack from Curley without resisting. (2) One of Lennie's eyes had been badly cut, a gash caused by Curley's swipe of a broken bottle across Lennie's jaw, and his face was bloodied, with red streaks like stripes down the right side. (3) At George's signal, Lennie grabbed in his huge hand Curley's fist in mid-punch, his strength now released through George's permission to retaliate, and held on with a steel grip. (4) Curley's face reddening, and his breath coming in short gasps, Lennie relentlessly tightened and squeezed the fist more and even more, until Curley was shaking uncontrollably from exploding pain in his shocked hand. (5) Ignoring Curley's agony, Lennie held Curley's fist like super-glue, but looked with childlike apprehension at George, glancing at him and seeking his approval and permission to retaliate by pulverizing Curley's hand, the fist that had so cruelly attacked him in his innocence and his mock defenselessness. (6) Abruptly, fearing Lennie would break Curley's hand, George yelled for Lennie to stop, but Lennie held tight, George's command barely penetrating Lennie's anger. (7) Curley's scream turned into a vanquished whimper, and Lennie, hearing the echo of George's command to stop and wanting to obey, let go. (8) Curley slumped to the ground, moaning.

EXAMPLE OF SEQUEL EVENT

Paragraph One: *Setting the Scene*

(1) In William Golding's novel *Lord of the Flies* a group of young boys, lost and isolated from society on a deserted island when their plane crashes, are forced to discover ways to survive and conduct society. (2) The plot focuses on two of those boys, Ralph and Jack, rivals for the leader of the boys. (3) At the end of the story, the boys are rescued and returned to civilization, but only after having formed warring tribes that descended into primitive, sometimes violent

behavior. (4) In the sample sequel paragraph below, the setting is some place in modern England, twenty years after the end of the novel. (5) For the first time since their rescue from the island, the adult Ralph and Jack, enemies on the island, meet.

Paragraph Two: *Describing the Scene*

Off Island

(1) Even though they had left it twenty years ago when the naval officer's cutter had saved them, it had never left their memory, flies buzzing around its hideously decomposing head, haunting all of them, but especially Ralph and Jack, with its recriminations of guilt, shame, and sudden, fierce, and naked awareness of the universal potential for evil. (2) The Lord of the Flies, outwardly a pig's head on a stake, had become for Ralph and Jack an internal voice of memory and of conscience, reminding them of their own savagery, intruding into their subsequent lives its nagging reminder of spears, of painted faces, of beasts within the darkness of jungle nights and within themselves, and of blood and death by violence. (3) Those memories had persisted over twenty years, immutably, like mountains. (4) And now, after twenty years of restless lives, their bodies no longer those of boys but of men, their minds still tainted with vestiges of childhood's fall from innocence, they looked at each other once again, listened to each other, but heard nothing except the echoing voice of the Lord of the Flies, a voice that they then only dimly but now unmistakably realized was their own. (5) Once again Ralph and Jack were together, the first time since the island. (6) It was a meeting both men had hoped would never happen, but an even more fervent hope required that it would. (7) This time there was no conch shell.

Choose one of these titles, or any other, to retell an event from the book, or create an event for a sequel to the book.

Animal Farm	*Slaughterhouse-Five*
A Farewell to Arms	*Siddhartha*
A Separate Peace	*The Autobiography of Malcolm X*
A Tale of Two Cities	*The Awakening*
Beloved	*The Chronicles of Narnia*
Brave New World	*The Color Purple*
Ethan Frome	*The Grapes of Wrath*
Gone with the Wind	*The Hobbit*
Great Expectations	*The Joy Luck Club*
Hawksong	*The Lord of the Rings*
Hiroshima	*The Metamorphosis*
I Know Why the Caged Bird Sings	*The Old Man and the Sea*
In Cold Blood	*The Pearl*
Jane Eyre	*The Red Pony*
Life of Pi	*The Stranger*
Lord of the Flies	*Their Eyes Were Watching God*
Of Mice and Men	*Things Fall Apart*
Oliver Twist	*To Kill a Mockingbird*
Pride and Prejudice	*Watership Down*
Roll of Thunder, Hear My Cry	*Wuthering Heights*

BECOMING A PRO!

Paragraphs for High School: A Sentence-Composing Approach is a collection of excellent sentences and paragraphs of pros—authors who are your mentors in good writing, and the best of all possible writing teachers.

Keep reading what they write, and learning how they write. Maybe you, too, can one day become a pro—and students will perhaps learn how to write from you as their mentor.

Whenever we read a sentence [or a paragraph], and like it, we unconsciously store it away in our model-chamber, and it goes, with the myriad of its fellows, to the building, brick by brick, of the eventual edifice which we call our style.

—Mark Twain

YOUR INVISIBLE TEACHERS

Approximately 300 titles were the basis for the activities in *Paragraphs for High School: A Sentence-Composing Approach*. Included were model sentences and paragraphs from hundreds of authors—your silent mentors, your invisible teachers. Here they all are, all of whom work hard at their craft to make reading easy for their readers.

I can't stand a sentence until it sounds right, and I'll go over it again and again. Once the sentence rolls along in a certain way, that's sentence A. Sentence B may work out well, but then its effect on sentence A may spoil the rhythm of the two together. One of the long-term things about knitting a piece of writing together is making all this stuff fit.

—John McPhee, author

In your writing, we hope all the stuff fits.

—The Killgallons

Aron Ralston, *Between a Rock and a Hard Place*
Alexander Dumas, *The Count of Monte Cristo*
Alexander Key, *The Forgotten Door*
Alice Munro, "The Office"
Alice Sebold, *The Lovely Bones*
Ambrose Bierce, "An Occurrence at Owl Creek Bridge"
Andre Agassi, *Open: An Autobiography*
Anne Morrow Lindbergh, *Gift from the Sea*

Anne Tyler, *The Amateur Marriage*

———, *Back When We Were Grownups*

———, *Saint Maybe*

Annie Dillard, *An American Childhood*

———, *Pilgrim at Tinker Creek*

Annie Proulx, "Man Crawling Out of Trees"

———, "The Wamsutter Wolf"

Arthur C. Clarke, *Dolphin Island*

Arthur Conan Doyle, *The Hound of the Baskervilles*

Audrey Niffenegger, *The Time Traveler's Wife*

Barack Obama, *Dreams from My Father*

Barbara Kingsolver, *Animal Dreams*

———, *Pigs in Heaven*

Bernard Malamud, "A Summer's Reading"

———, *The Fixer*

Betsy Byars, *The Summer of the Swans*

Bill and Vera Cleaver, *Where the Lilies Bloom*

Brian Greene, *The Parallel Reality*

Brian W. Aldiss, "Who Can Replace a Man?"

Carson McCullers, *The Member of the Wedding*

Charles Frazier, *Cold Mountain*

Christopher McDougall, *Born to Run*

Christopher Paolini, *Eragon*

Christy Brown, *My Left Foot*

Cormac McCarthy, *No Country for Old Men*

Cynthia Rylant, *Missing May*

Dan Dye and Mark Beckloff, *Amazing Gracie: A Dog's Tale*

Daoud Hari, *The Translator*

Dave Eggers, *A Heartbreaking Work of Staggering Genius*

David Wroblewski, *Edgar Sawtelle*

Diane Ackerman, *A Natural History of the Senses*

———, *The Zookeeper's Wife*

Dina Ingber, "Computer Addicts"

Dorothy Canfield, "The Heyday of the Blood"

Edgar Allan Poe, "The Cask of Amontillado"

Edward M. Kennedy, *True Compass*

Edward P. Jones, *Lost in the City*

Eleanor Coerr, *Sadako and the Thousand Paper Cranes*

Elizabeth Bowen, "Foothold"

Elizabeth Strout, *Olive Kitteridge*

Eric Larson, *The Devil in the White City*

Ernest Hemingway, *The Old Man and the Sea*

———, "The Undefeated"

Eugenia Collier, "Sweet Potato Pie"

Evan Connell, Jr., "The Condor and the Guests"

Fannie Flagg, *Standing in the Rainbow*

Frances Hodgson Burnett, *A Little Princess*

Francis Christensen, "A Generative Rhetoric of the Paragraph"

Frank Bonham, *Chief*

Frank McCourt, *Teacher Man*

Frank Norris, *McTeague*

Frank W. Dixon, *The Secret of the Old Mill*

Fred Gibson, *Old Yeller*

Fritz Leiber, "A Bad Day for Sales"

F. Scott Fitzgerald, *The Great Gatsby*

Garrison Keillor, *Pontoon*

Garth Stein, *The Art of Racing in the Rain*

Gary Paulsen, *Hatchet*

———, *The Time Hackers*

Gaston Leroux, *The Phantom of the Opera*

George Orwell, "A Hanging"

———, *1984*

Gerald Durrell, "The World in a Wall"

Gina Berriault, "The Stone Boy"

Gore Vidal, "Lincoln Up Close"

Greg Mortenson, *Three Cups of Tea*

Hal Borland, *When the Legends Die*

Harper Lee, *To Kill a Mockingbird*

Henry Sydnor Harrison, "Miss Hinch"

Hermann Hesse, *Siddhartha*

Howard Zinn, *A People's History of the United States*

Ian McEwan, *On Chesil Beach*

Isabel Allende, *Daughter of Fortune*

Jack London, *The Call of the Wild*

———, "To Build a Fire"

Jack Schaefer, *Shane*

James Baldwin, *Tell Me How Long the Train's Been Gone*

James Hilton, *Goodbye, Mr. Chips*

James Hurst, "The Scarlet Ibis"

James Joyce, "The Dead"

James Michener, *Centennial*

Jamie Ford, *The Hotel at the Corner of Bitter and Sweet*

J. D. Salinger, "De Daumier-Smith's Blue Period"

———, "Down at the Dinghy"

———, "The Laughing Man"

Jean Craighead George, *Julie of the Wolves*

———, *My Side of the Mountain*

Jean Shepherd, "A Fistful of Fig Newtons"

Jean Stafford, "Bad Characters"

Jeannette Walls, *Half Broke Horses*

———, *The Glass Castle*

Jeffrey Eugenides, *Middlesex*

Jessamyn West, "The Lesson"

Jhumpa Lahiri, *The Namesake*

———, *Unaccustomed Earth*

J. K. Rowling, *Harry Potter and the Chamber of Secrets*

———, *Harry Potter and the Deathly Hallows*

———, *Harry Potter and the Goblet of Fire*

———, *Harry Potter and the Half-Blood Prince*

Keith Donohue, *The Stolen Child*

Ken Follett, *The Pillars of the Earth*

Kenneth Brower, *The Starship and the Canoe*

Khaled Hosseini, *The Kite Runner*

Kim Edwards, *The Memory Keeper's Daughter*

Langston Hughes, "Road to Freedom"

Larry McMurtry, *Lonesome Dove*

Larry Weinberg, *Ghost Hotel*

Laura Hillenbrand, *Seabiscuit*

———, *Unbroken*

Lorrie Moore, *Self Help*

Leslie Marmon Silko, *Yellow Woman and a Beauty of the Spirit*

Leslie Morris, "Three Shots for Charlie Beston"

Lloyd Alexander, *The Book of Three*

Lois Lowry, *The Giver*

Madeleine L'Engle, *A Wrinkle in Time*

Malcolm X and Alex Haley, *The Autobiography of Malcolm X*

Margaret Landon, *Anna and the King of Siam*

Margaret Mitchell, *Gone with the Wind*

Marguerite Henry, *Misty of Chincoteague*

Mark Twain, *The Adventures of Tom Sawyer*

Mary Doria Russell, *Dreamers of the Day*

Marilynne Robinson, *Housekeeping*

Mark Haddon, *The Curious Incident of the Dog in the Night-Time*

Mary Ann Shaffer and Annie Barrows, *Guernsey Literary & Potato Peel Pie Society*

Maya Angelou, *The Heart of a Woman*

Meindert DeJong, *The Wheel on the School*

Michael Chabon, *The Amazing Adventures of Kavalier & Clay*

Michael Crichton, *Jurassic Park*

———, *Prey*

———, *Travels*

Mildred D. Taylor, *Let the Circle Be Unbroken*

————, *Roll of Thunder, Hear My Cry*

————, *Song of the Trees*

Mortimer Adler, "How to Mark a Book"

Murray Heyert, "The New Kid"

Nancy Hale, "You Never Know"

Natalie Babbitt, *Tuck Everlasting*

Neil Gaiman, *The Graveyard Book*

Norman Cousins, *Anatomy of an Illness*

Olive Ann Burns, *Cold Sassy Tree*

Oliver La Farge, "The Little Stone Man"

Oscar Hijuelos, *The Fourteen Sisters of Emilio Montez O'Brien*

Pat Conroy, *My Reading Life*

————, *South of Broad*

————, *The Prince of Tides*

Patricia MacLachlan, *Sarah, Plain and Tall*

Paul Harding, *Tinkers*

Paulo Coelho, *The Alchemist*

Perri Knize, *A Piano Odyssey*

Ray Bradbury, *Dandelion Wine*

————, "Kaleidoscope"

————, *The Martian Chronicles*

————, "There Will Come Soft Rains"

————, "The Whole Town's Sleeping"

Rebecca Skloot, *The Immortal Life of Henrietta Lacks*

Richard Lederer, "English Is a Crazy Language"

Richard Peck, *Those Summer Girls I Never Met*

Richard Wright, *American Hunger*

————, *Native Son*

Roald Dahl, *James and the Giant Peach*

————, *The BFG*

Robb White, *Deathwatch*

Robert C. O'Brien, *Mrs. Frisby and the Rats of NIMH*

Robert Cormier, *Take Me Where the Good Times Are*

Robert Lipsyte, *The Contender*
Robert Ludlum, *The Moscow Vector*
Robert Ramirez, "The Barrio"
Rosa Guy, *The Friends*
Roya Hakakian, *Journey from the Land of No*
Saki, "The Interlopers"
Sara Gruen, *Ape House*
———, *Water for Elephants*
Sarah Orne Jewett, "A White Heron"
Scott O'Dell, *Island of the Blue Dolphins*
Sheila Burnford, *The Incredible Journey*
Sherwood Anderson, "Unlighted Lamps"
———, *Winesburg, Ohio*
Shirley Jackson, "Charles"
———, "The Lottery"
Siddhartha Mukherjee, *The Emperor of All Maladies: A Biography of Cancer*
Sid Fleischman, *The Whipping Boy*
Sinclair Lewis, *Arrowsmith*
Stacy Schiff, *Cleopatra: A Life*
Stephen E. Ambrose, *Nothing Like It in the World*
Stephen King, *After Sunset*
———, *Bag of Bones*
———, *Carrie*
———, *Hearts in Atlantis*
———, *It*
———, *Just After Sunset*
———, *Needful Things*
———, *On Writing*
———, *The Eyes of the Dragon*
———, *The Stand*
Stephenie Meyer, *Twilight*
Steve Allen, "The Public Hating"
Steven Pinker, *The Language Instinct*

Stieg Larsson, *The Girl Who Kicked the Hornet's Nest*

———, *The Girl with the Dragon Tattoo*

Sue Miller, *While I Was Gone*

Susan Patron, *The Higher Power of Lucky*

Sylvia Plath, *The Bell Jar*

Tĕa Obreht, *The Tiger's Wife*

Theodore Taylor, *The Cay*

Thomas Wolfe, *Look Homeward, Angel*

Tobias Wolff, *Old School*

Tom Wolfe, *A Man in Full*

Toni Morrison, *Beloved*

———, *Song of Solomon*

Tracy Chevalier, *The Girl with a Pearl Earring*

Tracy Kidder, *Among Schoolchildren*

Truman Capote, "A Christmas Memory"

———, *In Cold Blood*

———, *The Grass Harp*

Virginia Woolf, "Lappin and Lapinova"

Wallace Stegner, *Crossing to Safety*

———, *Wolf Willow*

Walter Lord, *A Night to Remember*

W. H. Hudson, "Far Away and Long Ago"

Willa Cather, "The Sculptor's Funeral"

Willard Price, "The Killer Shark"

William Armstrong, *Sounder*

William Faulkner, "A Rose for Emily"

William Gibson, *Neuromancer*

William Golding, *Lord of the Flies*

William P. Young, *The Shack*

Yann Martel, *Beatrice and Virgil*

———, *Life of Pi*

*Writers learn to write by paying a certain sort of
attention to the works of their great and less great
predecessors in the medium of written language,
as well as by merely reading them.*

—*Toni Cade Bambara*, writer

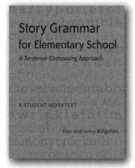